MO[illegible]
GHOSTLY

A. FARQUHARSON-COE

ISBN 0 904593 03 7

Distributed by Baron Jay Ltd.,
Publishers,
Faraday Road, Prince Rock,
Plymouth, PL4 0ST

It seems that all books have dedications, therefore to give this one every possible chance I dedicate it to my cat 'Patsy' but for whose 'help' it would have been finished very much sooner.

ACKNOWLEDGEMENTS

To the many friends who told me their own stories, or, in the tradition of legend, handed on to me, stories told them by their parents, grandparents or friends; to the Staff of the Local History Room at Plymouth Public Library. To the Western Morning News Ltd. for permission to reproduce their photograph of Childe's Tomb, and an extract from Miss Sylvia Calmady Hamlyn's article. To Messrs. Knight of Barnstaple for their photograph of Chulmleigh and to Mr. Haycock of Tavistock, who monitored the production of photographs for this and other books, my thanks.

TAVISTOCK A. FARQUHARSON COE

"I have milked many sources for this little book but the cheese is my own."

FOREWORD

In this dreary world of technique proliferation it is pleasant to realise that had I been born a few centuries earlier I would have been able to sit in the market place and tell old stories. To gather them together on paper is all that is left to me of that ancient freedom, and this I have done to the best of my ability. Many of the stories, particularly the ghost stories, are well known in Devon, but others, given me reluctantly under pledge of anonymity; were experienced by the tellers themselves and were still soaked in the horror of the happening, whatever may have been the truth of it.

The pages of the Western Morning News and the Transactions of the Devonshire Association proved fruitful sources of legends, but I used them as indicators, going to the district concerned and taking the story from its native soil. The genuine story is usually odd, the tiny growth of truth having been lopped and restored so often and so crudely over the years that today's version is almost always ludicrous, as in a famous Hampshire legend of a knight going dragon hunting with a sword in one hand and a jug of milk in the other! The complete stories, the tidy ones, such as that of Tamara's sad fate, the fairy bridge, and others like them, smack of nineteenth century preciosity, but who knows? .... they may avidly be sought for in the centuries to come, and it may have been my bounden duty to include them.

SIR WALTER RALEIGH'S GHOST STORY, OR THE TRUTH ABOUT TOBACCO

This story is derived from an old account, itself well over a hundred years old, of a fifteenth century ghost story. The reader should be prepared to have all his ideas about Sir Walter Raleigh's youthful ambitions, fostered no doubt by Millais's famous picture, rudely shattered. The earnest little boy so richly and unsuitably attired for sitting on a Devon beach was not being filled with dreams of empire building or gold hunting; he was trying to gather from the old yarn spinner's narrative some idea of where he ought to start looking for the herb tobacco. Far from discovering it himself he knew all about it from a story heard in his youth, long before he set sail for foreign parts. That story you are about to hear.

The scene is laid east of the river Exe and concerns the old church of St. John's-in-the-Wilderness, at what was then called Wythycombe Rawlegh and which is now a suburb of Exmouth. The church was in a ruinous state for many years and according to the story this was due to a vast concourse of 'Spirits and bogles' which frequented the building and the cemetery adjoining it. Attempts were made to destroy the building entirely after a chapel had been built to take its place, but all attempts to do so were abortive, being met with 'Dreadful disaster' so the old church was left to itself, its protection from natural decay being attributed to the old established evil influences. This church and its supernatural occupants was a great nuisance to the local family, the de Whalingham's who held the manor of Wythycombe Rawlegh, as this tale discloses.

Sir Roger de Whalingham was the lord of the manor of Wythycombe Rawlegh at this time and his immediate neighbour at Littleham was Sir Hugh de Creveldt, a knight of German descent. This gentleman could speak English and did so, but when moved to annoyance found English restrictive and swore in his native tongue. These two neighbours detested one another. Their tenants and servants also detested each other and fought whenever opportunity arose. Properly to understand the state of affairs at the time it must be realised that although such landowners were powerful and important people and were treated almost as gods by their tenantry and servants, they could be smugglers, wreckers and could turn beachcombers as readily as their tenants when their estates included a portion of the coast as did those of the two knights we are discussing.

Naturally in such an atmosphere of animosity the normal occupations of smuggling and beachcombing and the like meant almost daily battles. Matters between the two factions came to a head when a rich vessel from Genoa was wrecked, by act of God or assisted by the wreckers is not known.

The English knight, Sir Roger, and his servants got there first and secured a rich haul of velvets which Sir Roger greatly loved. All that was left for the German knight was a quantity of caviare, sixteen large jars of it. And he disliked caviare intensely. Almost as much as he loved Genoa velvet. He swore loud, and comprehensively in German, and after this incident the enmity between the two grew greater than ever before. In those days goblins demons and ghosts lived cheek by jowl with mankind so to speak; little reference was made to them even in bitter quarrels. Such things were not mentioned by reasonable men for fear of provoking these supernatural enemies. But the velvet and caviare business so incensed Sir Hugh that meeting Sir Roger one day he forsook his own tongue and abused him roundly in English, taunting him with the curse which lay on the de Whalingham family. He called him "The foul fiend of ghosts and goblins and the Wythycombe bogie feeder" ... This was insult indeed and unforgivable for the curse was a heavy burden on the family. The de Whalingham's were plagued every night of their lives with a visit from those ghosts and goblins which haunted the old church of St. John-in-the-Wilderness. This spectral crew descended upon the hall to demand seven musical requiems for the repose of their souls (apparently with little regard for that of their host). These seven masses were always sung, the ghosts and goblins themselves joining in. It was said that the nightly caterwauling could be heard all over the Exe valley.

Such a misfortune was hard enough to bear, but when the illiberal German knight threw in a vampire or two and reiterated the bogie feeder taunt, Sir Roger, worn out probably by the nocturnal howlings as well as the constant battle with his neighbour, turned on his tormentor and replied in measured and menacing tones "See to thyself, de Creveldt, that when my spirit leaves my body it visits thee not in thy fair domain of Littleham. It shall sit by thee in thy hall. It shall meet thee in thy walks. It shall draw the curtains of thy bed, till thou shall pray for the immortal spirits of Wythycombe to sing their requiem to its disturbed and wandering nature" ... That stopped

St. John's-in-the-Wilderness before restoration; from an old photograph

Sir Hugh in his tracks and although the hatred between them was as strong as ever, no word was spoken by either to the other from that day.

One stormy night in winter Sir Hugh was drowsing late in his chair before the fire, after a long day's hunting. Suddenly through the howling of the wind came the deep tones of the bell of Wythycombe Rawlegh's old church. This bell shared the supernatural mystery of the building. It had been taken to Italy and blessed by the Pope, and, like the famous bell in the cathedral of Saratoga, the bell of St. John's-in-the-Wilderness tolled for departing spirits without being touched by human hands. Sir Hugh, now thoroughly awake, listened, counting the bell strokes carefully. Should there be more than three the bell would be tolling for a passing parishioner of no great account, three strokes only meant a de Whalingham. Three sonorous tones sounded through the storm and ... no more! Apprehensively the knight leaped to his feet, straining to catch any possible further sound, made weaker by a sudden change in wind direction. Only the rain beat against the windows as the wind went howling round the house. Convinced that his old enemy was dead and remembering their last quarrel, he turned uneasily to the fireside. His blood froze. There, in his chair, sat Sir John de Whalingham, a cap from the famous velvet of Genoa upon his head. The two regarded one another, one with horror, the other impassively as befits a ghost. Neither spoke nor moved. At the end of the hour the ghost vanished 'With a slight musical sound' .. which the narrator informs us is always made by a ghost as it compresses itself to pass through a keyhole.

From thenceforward the old squire of Wythycombe Rawlegh kept his promise. Three times during every twenty-four hours his ghost appeared to his old neighbour at Littleham. One hour during his walks, one hour during the night and one hour at meals. And it was at meals that the ghost took his utmost revenge for the years of enmity between them. Each dish, as it was placed before de Creveldt, was instantly whisked away and a plate of the detested caviare substituted. In vain every available source of supply of the commodity was stopped, the ghost seemed to have an inexhaustible stock. The poor knight grew weak and ill. In vain his huntsmen tried to lure him to the chase, in vain his daughter plied her lute. Sir Hugh pined away until he was practically a wandering skeleton, and it was when his life was almost at an end that an old friend of his, a captain of a trading vessel, visited him. His name was Isaackes and he had newly arrived from Cadiz, anchoring his vessel in the estuary of the Exe. Meeting de Creveldt he was horrified at the change in him. The knight poured out the whole story and when it was finished the old sailor sat for a long time in thought.

Suddenly, leaping from his chair, he cried,

"I have it Sir Knight, I have it! .. We will smoke him out!"

The dejected knight expostulated saying that the ghost himself was nothing but smoke or vapour. "So much the better" replied the other. "Two of a kind can never agree" .. He then proceeded to describe the properties of the Indian weed as he called tobacco, which had been brought to Europe by some of the seamen accompanying the great Columbus. As it happened he had a supply of the stuff in his own ship.

For want of a better solution to his troubles de Creveldt gave his old friend a free hand and the captain set to work. Next day, after the ghost had paid his morning visit, the captain sealed up every crevice and cranny in the dining hall in order that neither ghost nor smoke should escape before the latter had done its work. When the hall was effectually caulked as the captain described it, the time was approaching for the ghost's mealtime appearance. Promptly as the knight's portion of curlew pie was placed before him, the plate was snatched away and the caviare made its usual appearance. The meal continued and when it had been cleared away the ghost lingered for its usual time then prepared to depart. Our nineteenth century narrator breaks off to inform us that 'spectres breathe only pure oxygen without azote' mere mortals apparently being obliged to sustain life upon a mixture. The reader will observe that science had begun to raise its miserable head into this ancient story, although we may be thankful that spectres are still permitted us. To continue .. the ghost prepared to depart but found its keyhole blocked.

Meanwhile the two mortals had produced 'tubes' and lighted their tobacco which must have been some pretty crude stuff. The ghost went round and round, seeking another way out as the room rapidly filled with dense clouds of tobacco smoke. The poor spirit was soon lost to view but it is remarked that the rustling of his velvets was still heard (how that successful bit of beachcombing seems to have rankled!) Soon the poor ghost was visited with a storm of sneezes and sternutations as our scientifically minded narrator tells us, but the two smoked on.

How the unfortunate de Creveldt fared in his first attempt at smoking in his weakened state is not known, but as the story goes on to say that Captain Isaackes persisted in smoking his tobacco without reference to his fellow conspirator it almost looks as if the latter had fallen by the wayside and was in as bad a case as the ghost.

Eventually before the kippering process was complete, a weak hollow groan was heard and the spectre begged for the door to be opened. He was a wordy fellow even at the point of dissolution. "If thou wilt once open the door" he moaned "I will haunt thee no more. Destroy me thou canst not. The poisonous vapour may affect my aerial substance" – an understatement one feels considering the frightful fug there must have been in that place, but the circumambient Victorian science coloured the spirit's despair no doubt ... "Me it cannot annihilate!" A nasty word to say amid sneezes and sternutations. A meaningful dialogue ensued and eventually the spirit undertook to leave off haunting and lunch lifting. The door was opened and all parties adjourned to the fresh air.

And that, dear reader, according to the nineteenth century narrator is the real story of how tobacco came to England. When the last of the de Whalingham's died, Sir Walter Raleigh's family, already domiciled in the neighbourhood, acquired the estate. It is said that the young Sir Walter was so intrigued and obsessed with this ancient ghost story that, as soon as he could, he set off for Virginia to acquire some of this potent ghost destroying weed, and all the stories of statesmanship, poetry writing, cloak laying and similar activities are merely by the way.

KEEPER OF THE GATE

Bere Alston is in the famous Tamar Valley, and Braunder Farm is not far from the river itself, but between the farm and the village lies the local big house, an elegant eighteenth century building set in parkland. It is now used as a school, the fate of many such beautiful houses in these days. Two gateways, side by side, give access to the grounds. One is the gate to the drive leading to the front of the house, the other road runs to the back of the house and then on to the road to the village. The gate to this road is nearly always open. It was open one still, cold, winter night when about eight thirty, Mr. Wager from Braunder Farm drove down to pick up his wife who was visiting a friend in the big house. As he neared the gateway, making no attempt to slacken speed, he was horrified to see a

The haunted gateway

dwarfish shape about three feet high detach itself from the hedge behind the gate and slam it shut in his path. The thing then disappeared back into the hedge.

Mr. Wager braked hard, and when he had regained his composure and mobility courageously left the car and opened the gate. He searched the hedge as far as his headlights illuminated it but saw no break or disturbance in the thick hawthorn growth. Neither did he see any trace of the churlish shape. Driving down to the house he picked up his wife and returned through the gateway, the gate being still open as he had left it.

Some time later, when he could bring himself to discuss the incident he discovered that something queer was known about the gate but no one seemed to know exactly what it was or any story to account for the dislike in which it was held. Pondering on the incident Mr. Wager recalled an old man who used the same gate and roadway on journeys to the village inn. Never would he start the journey back from the village between eight and ten at night. If ready to start before eight, off he went. If not, he waited until ten o'clock and then set off along the road. Had he, wondered Mr. Wager, once met that awful little shape and dreaded a re-encounter? .. If so, he had kept his own counsel but took no further chances.

The big house itself was not free from terror. Unaccountably Mrs. Wager disliked ascending the wide staircase. There could, of course, have been many quite innocent causes for this fear. The stealthy sounds of fabric settlement in an old house and its many but indefinite echoes are enough to disturb even the most prosaic person in a large and underoccupied building. Mrs. Wager's fears were justified however one day when she and her friend were ascending the staircase. Down from the upper floor swept an unseen but violent presence, brushing roughly between the two women and pushing them to each side of the stairway. Even of this phenomenon there seems to be no previous history.

By contrast Braunder's own ghost is a delightfully friendly dog. In life she belonged to Mr. Wager and was called Lassie. One sad day Lassie became embroiled in a fight and was so badly injured that she died. Some time later Mrs. Wager was standing at the kitchen sink engaged in the unimaginative task of washing dishes, when she was surprised to feel a gentle brushing across the back of her legs, such as a dog makes with its gently moving tail. Twice she felt this invisible tail movement and could only conclude that Lassie had returned and was greeting her mistress in her old affectionate manner. Later a visitor to the house who knew nothing of the dog or its tragic end, felt the same gentle tail brush against her skirt. Somewhat hesitantly, anticipating possible ridicule no doubt, she related her experience to her hosts, to be told of the dog's death and of what Mr. and Mrs. Wager feel convinced was her earlier visit to her old home.

RICHARD BOVET'S STORIES

In 1696 a trial of a witch was held in Exeter before Sir John Holt. Those troublous times saw many such trials but this one ended rather more happily than most; the witch was acquitted. Perhaps the evidence against old Bess Horner was too ridiculous, even for the credulity of the seventeenth century. Her alleged victims were three children who were said to have performed the most absurd actions, including walking up walls to the height of nine feet, where they remained, swearing that Bess Horner was holding them there. Pin spitting, a recognised activity in those bewitched, was indulged in by these children practically continually, and one of them swore that Bess carried a large toad on her shoulder wherever she went. But in spite of all these stories Sir John directed the jury to acquit the old lady, which was done.

Now the name of the complainant, the father of the children, was William Bovet, and nothing other than his appearance in this case seems to have been recorded about him. However, in 1684, twelve years before Bess Horner was tried at Exeter, a Richard Bovet wrote a book which was very rare, even in the nineteenth century when the account from which these particulars were taken was written. In this book there is ample evidence that the writer was a West countryman and that he was a fanatical enemy of what he called popery and witchcraft, lumping the two activities together in his book and railing against both to his utmost ability. He refers in it to an account of the behaviour of what he terms 'the Demon of Spraiton' (presumably Spreyton) which was written in the year 1683, the lunatic ongoings of which he declares were known to the minister of Barnstaple. The Demon story follows.

In November 1682 an employee of a landowner named Philip Furze was walking over his master's fields when he was accosted by what Mr. Bovet refers to as a 'Resemblance' – what we should call a ghost – of an old man, his master's old father who had recently died. The employee, whose name was

Fey, noticed that the apparition carried a staff or stick which established his identity in Fey's mind as the old man always carried such a stick for the purpose of killing moles as he walked round the fields when he was alive.

The old ghost seemed perturbed that certain legacies and bequests he had made in his will had not been paid to the beneficiaries. One item, which seemed to upset him particularly, was a sum of twenty shillings which he told Fey to obtain from his executor, the old man's son and Fey's master. He was to carry it to his sister, Philip Furze's aunt, who lived at Totnes. If this could be done he promised to give no further trouble. Unluckily, his business being concluded, the ghost lingered awhile, chatting to the young man, and incidentally reviling his second wife in no uncertain terms. That lady was dead. Eventually he disappeared, but the harm was done.

Young Fey did as he was bidden and rode with the money to Totnes. The old lady, however, refused to accept it when she heard what had happened, saying that she was afraid it might have come from the Devil, which seems rather uncomplimentary to the old ghost. He was compelled to materialise again to instruct the young man to obtain a ring from a Totnes jeweller for the lady undertaking that she would accept this, which she did. Poor young Fey could be forgiven for thinking, as he rode homeward, that he had brought matters to a satisfactory conclusion. He was not to think so for long. When he arrived at Spreyton the old man's second wife's apparition appeared, leaping on the horse behind him. Irritated no doubt by her husband's unchivalrous remarks to the young man on the occasion of his first appearance and irrationally blaming him for listening to them perhaps, she threw poor young Fey from his horse. As soon as he remounted she threw him to the ground again. From then on this lovable lady stayed around, sometimes in her old earth shape, sometimes in the shape of a large and savage dog which galloped about breathing and belching fire. To vary the performance she turned herself into a horse, but with uncharacteristic consideration only displaced a small pane of glass when, in equine shape, she chose to jump through a window.

The young man got no peace from this she devil. She half strangled him with his own handkerchief and cravat. She wedged him into the narrow space between the wall and his bed. She tore his wigs from his head and destroyed them before his eyes, finally bewitching his shoe strings so that they wriggled away from him like snakes and he could not catch them. On days when she could think of nothing better (or worse) to do she picked him up and tossed him into the nearest bog. So distressed did the poor young fellow become that he had to be taken to a doctor at Crediton to be bled. Left in a room by himself for a few minutes he was found bruised and 'in one of his fits' (Is this the clue, was the unfortunate young man an epileptic?) On recovering his senses he swore that a large bird had flown in through the window, carrying a stone in its beak with which it beat him over the head. The room was searched and a large weight made of brass and copper was found which was immediately seized upon by the on-lookers and broken up for souvenirs.

This story ended, and what happened to the unfortunate Fey is never revealed, Richard Bovet then gives an account of the happenings when he went to stay 'At the house of a nobleman' a house which he says used to be a nunnery. It is a pity that he does not give its name. The house was full and Bovet was compelled to share a room with a gentleman whom he refers to as Mr. C. The two were lying in bed, idly chatting before they went to sleep when, says Bovet, he became aware of what he calls an 'Appearance' of a well dressed and beautiful lady, followed by four more such. They walked quietly round the room then the leader came to Bovet's bedside and gently touched his hand. He called to Mr. C. to ascertain if he also saw the visitors, whereupon they all vanished. Rising he went over to Mr. C's bed to find out why he had not replied. He found him absolutely unable to move or speak and stiff with fright. When he recovered Mr. C. said that while his friend was being patted by the beautiful lady he was being menaced by a dreadful monster at the bottom of his bed. It was shaped like a lion and was trying to scramble upon the bed when Mr. Bovet spoke then it disappeared.

The next night Bovet was visited by an invisible lady who was dressed he asserted, in a tabby gown, a material he recognised by its rustle as she paced round the room. He heard her hook a foot under the rail of a chair and drag it round the room with her. She then took a large book and sat rustling its leaves, punctuating her studies with lugubrious groans. Nothing else seems to have happened that night, but it is an account of the next night's performance which must make us wonder if his hosts or their servants were indulging in what we would term leg pulling. He tells us with all solemnity that a footman was going to bed when two beauteous she spirits assailed him. One snatched the bedclothes from his bed, the other grabbed his nightshirt as he was trying to put it on, running off with it so that the poor fellow was left naked. One spirit then tried to scramble on to the bed with him and when he fought her off, the other leaped at him from the other side, and in this atmosphere of nineteenth century French farce the story ends.

These are the experiences Bovet said he had had, or appeared ready to believe when others claimed to have had them. After these, old Bess Horner's efforts even if true, seem small beer indeed. Richard Bovet seems to have been a fairly well known personage in the West, writers not being so thick on the ground then as now. Could it not be that the family of Bovet and its reputation was known to Sir John and influenced his decision to ask for Bess Horner's acquittal.

THE LUFFINCOTT RECTORY

The rector who was terrified out of the rectory was appointed in 1904 and resigned his living in 1906. His name was Browne and he was a bachelor and partially paralysed, poor man. It is difficult to decide why the apparition who so frightened him chose this young bachelor clergyman to terrify, for two rectors had officiated at Luffincott between 1883 when the Reverend Parker, whose ghost did the frightening, died, and 1904 when Mr. Browne came to the parish. The Reverend Franke Parker was also a bachelor and it may be that his two successors had wives whose presence discouraged his ghost from trying any terrifying in their time. The old man loved his rectory and was often heard to declare that he felt the place really belonged to him. He was a rich man and employed a full staff of servants. Also he was believed to have an interest in magic for he possessed a large quantity of mysterious books he forbade his servants to touch. Anything kept secret in those days meant witchcraft, or some other dark occupation.

The Reverend Browne was a very different person. He had no money for expensive service and looked after himself. He probably quite enjoyed himself living alone and reading at meals whenever he wished. It was when he was so occupied that he happened to glance up from his book to see the Reverend Franke standing before him. That much he was induced to tell but no one knew what happened or what the ghost had said which caused the poor man to bolt out of his rectory and never return to it. Not only did he refuse to return but he would not allow his belongings to be brought from it. He returned to his lodgings at Clawton where he had been curate and drove over to Luffincott to discharge his parochial duties, eating his lunch while sitting in the church porch, continuing in this way until he resigned the living at Luffincott.

That the ghost the rector had seen was that of the Reverend Franke Parker was established, when a photograph was shown to him, which included the figure of the old man. He recognised it at once, and that is all that the most indefatigable gossip could discover. That the new rector had seen the ghost of the old and would not risk repeating the experience. Granted that those were the days when orthodox religion had a much stronger hold on men than it has today, with the corresponding horror of the power of a curse, particularly one uttered by a priest (or his ghost) and such a rich and awe inspiring one as the Reverend Franke seems to have been in his time. The young bachelor priest, so lately a curate, was no doubt a sensitive soul and perhaps a tiny bit overwhelmed by the sudden acquisition of a rectory, but all that should not have made him scream and run away, which he is said to have done when he was confronted with a picture of the Reverend Franke.

Naturally, when the story got around, the inquisitive members of the congregation made their way to the abandoned rectory, in broad daylight no doubt and in company, to view the scene of the crime as it were, and as the news of the rector's determination never to go there again spread around the parish, people entered through doors and windows and took 'souvenirs'. Soon there was little or nothing left to take away, and wayfarers began to use the old rectory as a posting house, undeterred by the possibility of seeing the old rector's ghost. As so often happens with abandoned houses, and careless tramps, the old rectory of Luffincott was burned down.

THE GHOSTS AT THE NEWSAGENTS

Cowick Street is in a haunted district of Exeter, modernise it as you will. St. Thomas's Church is not far away, and the old monastic foundation of St. Thomas was in that neighbourhood. St. Thomas's own ghosts still walk, we meet them later; the ghosts with which we are concerned here, haunted the more prosaic surroundings of a newsagent's and stationer's shop in Cowick Street, and, until they were invited into the open, seem to have been content to remain in hibernation.

The shop in question had been in the occupation of the same family since 1917 but the family name, Perriam, has been a well known one in the county since a very much earlier date. Our ghost story starts with the day when Mrs. Perriam and her mother-in-law were discussing the question of space for stock, always a problem for shopkeepers but a particularly difficult one with dealers in such bulky merchandise as that with which these ladies were concerned. A cupboard under the stairs seemed the only unexplored possibility. These understair cupboards are fairly general in buildings and have a limited use, for often there is no light and little ventilation in them. But they have some use and Mrs. Perriam was at a loss to understand why this one had been securely fastened and sealed. In some inexplicable way she found this perfectly ordinary looking cupboard door disquieting. It seemed to have something queer and frightening about it. But the stock for which they wanted space had to go somewhere and finally it was decided that this cupboard under the stairs should be opened.

A dark, ill-ventilated space cannot be a welcoming spectacle, but when the door was eventually unfastened after much effort, the spooky feeling of horror which swept over the women was unnerving; what presented itself was horrific. A spectral face, that of an aged man, almost skeletal, leered at them for a terrifying second, then vanished. From then on, mysterious knocks were heard with no human agency to account for them. There was more to come. A black boy appeared through a window, to move noiselessly along a passage, although this visitor was so beautiful that the lady who saw him was in no way frightened.

There seems to be no history to account for these mysterious happenings triggered off by the opening of the understair cupboard, though there must have been some reason for the very efficient sealing. The building was formerly part of the old Black Horse Inn, which may have had something to do with the trouble.

The newsagency has now been sold and Mrs. Perriam has left the district. The new proprietors have had a few strange experiences, including the behaviour of their dog who spent one night barking for some unaccountable reason. This dog was an unusually silent animal; had always been so and never had been known to bark at night, but not long after he came to live in his new home the dog, who slept in the kitchen, began to bark furiously one night. Of course noises strange to the animal but quite usual in the new neighbourhood could have startled it, but to hear such a placid animal apparently frightened into making such a noise was an eerie experience to the dog's owners.

The fateful staircase cupboard door has been sealed for good this time and the shop has been altered and enlarged. Nothing has been heard or seen of the ghosts, and it must be assumed that they went out with the building debris.

SPECTRAL HOUNDS, AND OTHER DOGS

Black dogs can be considered a Scandinavian importation into Britain although there are stories of Celtic hounds, but these are believed to be white or pale coloured creatures. The Scandinavians were Odin's Hounds, and their phantom progeny in packs and individually, roam over moor and meadow, lane, park and woodland, all over the kingdom. They tear over Dartmoor on wild windy nights, hunted by the Devil, or trot behind the same gentleman as he takes them back from exercise to their kennel in Wistman's Wood. They are Whisht Hounds if they hunt the southern part of the moor and if they are seen in the north they are referred to as Yeth Hounds.

Sir Francis Drake is believed to have returned in spectral form, not at the summoning roll of his drum to preserve England from danger, but to hunt a pack of these black hounds in the vicinity of his old home, Buckland Abbey. The hounds which raced down from Dartmoor to rage round the house when Squire Cabell lay duing at his home near Buckfastleigh, were also black. It is more than likely that these hounds were his own, and no phantoms; for Squire Cabell, beside being the district's bete noire himself, was a great hunting man and kept a pack of black hounds. In the north it is, or was, the custom to keep what, if I remember rightly, used to be called a trencherfed pack; the hounds lodged with whoever would feed and shelter them, mustering to the sound of the horn in the village street on hunting days and returning to base at the end of the day's sport. It is possible that Squire Cabell kept his black hounds on the same principle. They would know in the mysterious way dogs have, of their master's impending death, and just one howl would set off the rest. The racing and fire belching were probably the artistic additions of a superstitious neighbourhood.

The tales of single black dogs, hounds, or what you will, met with on Dartmoor are many and varied in horror. There is the story of the man who set out to walk from Princetown to Plymouth who was accosted, if that is the right term, by a large black dog of the retriever type. Putting down his hand to pat the animal, for he liked dogs, the poor man was horrified to find his hand passing through the animal's head. Nevertheless man and dog walked along together until they reached a particular corner. Here the dog became aggressive and refused to allow the man to pass on. Eventually the poor fellow managed to evade the dog and made a short run, only to find the dog flying at his throat. He fought it off and staggered on a few yards where he collapsed. Later it was ascertained that many years previously a man was murdered at this corner, his large black retriever being the only witness of the tragedy. Ever since that day the valiant dog has been trying, by what seems a process of elimination, to find the murderer and avenge his master.

Another man who met the same dog was so terrified when his attempt to caress the creature met thin air, that he broke into a run. The dog kept beside him in an effortless silent lope until they reached the crossroads. As the dog turned to fly at the man there was a sudden blinding flash of light and the poor fellow dropped unconscious. When he recovered he found himself lying in the road, alone, with no sign of his assailant.

Many years ago a black dog as large as a donkey used to haunt the Postbridge district, but this animal has not been seen for many a year. The black hound which haunted a lane in Bradworthy has not been seen for over seventy years, for which no doubt the parish is grateful for the animal's appearance always meant bad luck. Farther north and to the east, Sir Robert Chichester of Martinhoe is said to roam in the shape of a black dog, varying the performance by reverting to his own human form now and then. On these occasions he rides in a flaming coach drawn by four elephants.

To vary the colour if not the subject a little, there are stories of white hounds being seen on other parts of Dartmoor. One young man was driving on the A30 one dark night when a large pale dog as big as a Great Dane suddenly appeared in his headlights. Convinced that he must have hit it he stopped the car and searched the road but there was no sign of a dog. But this is not mystifying; if a dog is hurt but not crippled, he puts as much distance as possible as quickly as possible between himself and his injurer. Or he gets to cover. But these are ghost stories and we must be impractical. A white hound also appears near Widecombe, but there is no doubt about this one. It responds to advances but disappears just when the observer feels he is making headway with the animal.

Black dogs, hounds or otherwise, attend practically every reputable ghost in Devon. Lady Howard is said to be accompanied by one or a pack of them on her drives to Okehampton, and the old Colonel's coach driving along the lanes near Ashburton has a couple of escorting black hounds. Sir Francis Drake naturally has his share and black hounds escort him on his drives to Plymouth or other local places of interest (to him) in his coach drawn by headless horses. It is very easy to identify his hounds for they, like the horses are headless.

BERRY POMEROY GHOSTS

Some Devon ghost stories are famous all over Britain and the story of Sir William Farquhar's sighting of the famous Berry Pomeroy lady ghost is one of them. Who could doubt the word of a physician of such standing; the Queen's own physician, and a very sensible well balanced gentleman at that.

The story starts when a lady, the wife of the Castle steward lay ill at Berry Pomeroy Castle and Sir William then staying in the neighbourhood was asked to pay her a professional visit. Admitted to the castle by a servant he was asked to wait in a small parlour while the patient's husband was informed of his arrival. As he waited he was surprised to see the door open silently and a lady, young and in great distress, walk across the room and mount a small circular staircase which rose from a corner of it. She was very beautiful and Sir William was greatly moved. He spoke to her, but received no reply as she vanished round the corner of the staircase. He was then called to the patient, who was so ill that all thought of the damsel in distress went from his mind. He treated the lady and prescribed medicines, saying that he would call the following day. This he did and to his relief found the patient much better. He was leaving the Castle escorted by the patient's grateful husband when he remembered the weeping lady and he asked what had caused her distress and whether she was a member of the family. To his consternation the steward who had been chatting quite happily in view of his wife's recovery, showed sudden horror. His face became ashen as he murmured brokenly "Now I know my wife will die. That was the ghost and she always appears before a death at Berry Pomeroy!" To Sir William this was sheer nonsense in view of the marvellous progress the patient had made in so short a time, pointing out that the wife had practically recovered and a few more days would see her completely restored to health. The husband refused to be comforted, and seeing all effort would be useless in the face of such a deeprooted superstition, he left the Castle.

The following day, news was brought that the lady had had a sudden relapse during the night and had died before help could be obtained.

This is the ghost story which was vouched for by Sir William Farquhar. Another story which may have some connection with his, concerns the ghost of a beautiful young lady known as Lady Margaret who stands on a ruined staircase and beckons to visitors. But between the beautiful apparition and the visitor is a chasm caused by the ruins of the lower part of the staircase, a circular stone staircase, into which the unwary stranger falls should he accept the lady's gesture of invitation and approach her. Could it not be the same staircase, and the lady's tears turned to smiles for the occasion?

There are many other stories of Berry Pomeroy, some of them rather horrible. One story, rather more pleasant than the others concerns the old gateway of the Castle. Near it lie the remains of an old pleasaunce and there, in an ancient arbour hidden by summer leaves, a daughter of the house used to meet a young man who, unfortunately was an hereditary enemy of her house. Enraged by the sight of this perfidy, the girl's brother, stealing upon the unsuspecting pair one day, drew his sword and slew them both. Now, in a small recess in a tortuous passage inside the Castle entrance, when the summer moon is full, the shadowy forms of the young lovers stretch loving arms to each other, arms which never meet for the malevolence of Pomeroy hatred which killed them keeps them apart.

THE GHOST IN THE FLATS

Abbotskerswell lies between Newton Abbot and the sea and one of the important houses there in the old days was Aller House. It was turned into flats some years ago, the fate of many a lovely old house in these disastrous days, and in 1963 a young couple moved into one of the two ground floor flats. They were probably delighted to have a home of their own, and for a week or so they were allowed to possess it in peace; then a poltergeist joined them. Furniture was shaken in a peculiar way ornaments moved of their own accord and crockery flew from the shelves. This continued for some time, then one night in the dim light from a half opened door, the young husband saw the shadowy outline of a man, an outline that gradually faded as he watched.

By this time the two young people were badly shaken, but flats were hard to come by and they tried to ignore their unwelcome guest, but when the wardrobe started shaking one night and then moved out bodily into the room they had had enough. Next day they moved out. Several times they tried to return to the flat but the disturbances drove them out, and in the end they gave the ghost his way and left him in possession.

When the tenants of the first flat were away, the occupants of the other ground floor flat said that they had been disturbed by noises, although they knew that the other flat was unoccupied. Before giving up altogether the first young couple went to the vicar of the parish to ask his advice. The vicar arranged with the Bishop of Exeter for the Bishop's chaplain to visit the house and give his opinion on the trouble. A meeting was held in the flat at which the tenant, the vicar and the chaplain were present. So was the ghost according to the tenant, who said he always knew when the ghost was in the room although he did not always see him. The chaplain said he felt cold and apprehensive and could not rid himself of the feeling, but the vicar confessed to feeling quite warm and comfortable.

On receiving his chaplain's report the Bishop came to Aller House and conducted a service of exorcism. The tenant said afterward that 'Albert' as the ghost had been nicknamed, stood quietly behind the Bishop for most of the service but disappeared before it was over. On record it was believed that the ghost gave no more trouble, but the tenants insisted that this was not so. In December, after the first couple had left, the ghost made his appearance in the other flat. The husband had been sitting late over some work on his ledgers when he began to feel chilled and uneasy. Looking over his shoulder he was terrified to meet the gaze of a man about forty, dressed in clothes of an Edwardian fashion, who stood quietly behind him. The man vanished but not before the flat owner had time to notice that he was quite goodlooking and seemed to be regarding him with a wistful pensive air.

By this time a considerable amount of interest had been aroused and previous tenants came forward to say that they had felt uneasy and uncomfortable in the house and eventually left it, although they had had no manifestations or supernatural interference of any kind to cause them to leave. For some time the house was used as an office for a business making glue and other by products of a knackers' yard which was conducted in the buildings. The manager of this business had killed himself when an investigation of the books was proposed. Whether this was the ghost who so disturbed the flat dwellers cannot be decided, for it was said that a previous owner of the house also committed suicide. However, the end of the 1960's saw the demolition of this unhappy house and presumably the ghosts went with it.

LYDFORD'S BLACK PIG AND GORGE

Where possible I have tried always to get first hand stories in this book. It is not always easy and I was delighted when I came upon someone who could assure me that he had seen the Black Pig of Lydford Castle. He saw it one night when he had just left that delightful inn 'The Castle' which is close to the dour old keep which is all that remains of Lydford Castle. Alas my delight was slightly diminished when one of his friends added that on that occasion the young man was in such a condition that he would have seen anything. However the Black Pig has been seen on many occasions and it is believed that the creature is the earthbound spirit of the ill-famed Judge Jefferys. History insists that Judge Jefferys did not officiate at Lydford in any capacity. I have always thought that the Black Pig if he exists in the world of phantoms must be the wraith of Sir Richard Grenville who was in charge of the affairs of Lydford in the seventeenth century. He was a cruel vindictive man. If he treated his prisoners as he treated his wife, the unfortunate Lady Howard, who married him as her fourth husband, he deserves to haunt that dreary fortress for ever.

Lydford Gorge in the sixteenth and seventeenth centuries was the home of a gang of bandits, thieves and murderers whose depredations so tormented the people of the district that in the end its inhabitants banded together, hunted them out and destroyed them as vermin. They lived in holes in the ground, living as animals without animal dignity. These people were known as the Gubbinses and were led by a particularly vicious character named Roger Rowly. Many horrible stories are told of their doings and Lydford must have been greatly relieved when they were finally destroyed.

The gorge at Lydford is a gem of magnificent scenery if one has a good head for heights and is surefooted. There is a spectacular waterfall and a weird and haunted pool where the ghost of an old woman, who is said to have fallen from the slippery path to her death in the pool on her way home from market, appears beside it on the anniversary of her death. Other fatalities have occurred in the gorge, one of the latest being the drowning of a young soldier whose body was discovered in the pool weeks after his disappearance. A grim and gruesome spot.

VIOLENCE AT SAMPFORD PEVERELL

Sampford Peverell's vicar in the early nineteenth century was a conscientious clergyman who took his parishioners' troubles seriously; he contributed a substantial sum to a reward which was offered for the discovery of the cause of poltergeist activity in a prominent villager's house. This man was a Mr. Chave who was tormented by a poltergeist who spent its time slamming hammerblows into a bed which seemed to have annoyed it. The noise created was like that of a very heavy fist or mallet, and the vicar counted more than two hundred blows on one occasion. The bed curtains were shaken, the rings rattling like castanets, and the performance finished with a noise of fabric being torn. Afterwards a long rent was found across the weave of the heavy curtains.

Doors had to be opened with care for the opener was apt to be startled by loud blows or raps on the far wall as he entered. When the vicar entered one room he was greeted with so much tumult from walls and ceiling that the place seemed to be collapsing round his ears.

Nothing in the way of an apparition seems to have been seen by Mr. Chave or the vicar, but a young labourer swore that he had seen the figure of a woman accompanied by what he termed a "thumping noise" followed by a sound like thunder in the room with him. Six women servants working at varying times in the house swore that they had been beaten until they were numb when they slept in the attics and were sore for many days afterward. One, a young girl, said that she had been struck on the cheek while lying in bed, the blow raising a swelling as large as an egg.

The vicar conducted several experiments to discover the cause of the trouble. He laid a heavy sword and a massive bible on the bottom of the offending bed, and, with two independent witnesses standing by, waited to see what would happen. The poltergeist did not keep them waiting for long. Contemptuously he tossed the things across the room to crash against the wall seven feet away. Naturally the maidservants were terrified and one night two of them were so frightened that they refused to remain in their attic bedroom any longer. Trooping downstairs they beat on the door of their master's room and begged to be taken in. Mr. Chave and his wife arose and made a makeshift bed for the women in the corner of the room and all tried to return to slumber. The poltergeist seems to have accompanied his victims for the slamming and banging started afresh in Mr. Chave's room. The poor man lit a candle to ring the bell for assistance from the men servants. Hardly had he done so before the light was blown out and the heavy iron candlestick snatched from him and thrown into his face.

The owner of the house is said to have spread the idea that Mr. Chave wished to buy the house and was inventing these stories so that he could get it cheaply, but the vicar said that this could not possibly be true. The property was entailed and the owner only a tenant for life. He could not have sold the house even had he wished. Other villagers said that the vicar, whose brother was believed to be one of the smuggling clergymen of the south coast of Devon, was in the scheme with Mr. Chave and that the house at Sampford Peverell was being used as a smuggler's cache. Certainly there was a kind of secret chamber under the floor boards of the most haunted room. It was duly inspected and showed no sign of having been used for years.

The noises and disturbances continued from about 1810 until 1813 then gradually faded away ... There is no record that anyone attempted to claim the reward.

THE BLACK HOUSE OF BRIXHAM

This famous house in Brixham is believed to have been a monastic establishment dating from the fourteenth century. The ghost there has a playful habit of locking people into the bathroom. The story of the ghost and his place of haunt is an example of pathetically wasteful parental interference. Only think! If a tyrannical father had not interfered with the matrimonial arrangements of his son, he would not now have to wander in ghostly shape seeking him to ask his forgiveness. Which seems unreasonable because the son should also be in the world of restless spirits for he killed himself because of his sire's interference. Which of them does the bathroom locking business is not known.

BETSY OF TAVISTOCK

Betsy Grimbal is Tavistock's own ghost. She is believed to be the ghost of a nun who loved a monk in those misty days known as 'long ago'. The monk, it is said, wearied of her and eventually murdered poor Betsy. Another version states that Betsy was murdered by a soldier; yet another implicates that aristocratic scapegoat, Lady Howard, who murdered either one of her husbands or a daughter in that ruinous tower beside the Bedford Hotel.

Whoever she was in life, in ghosthood Betsy takes her position in Tavistock very seriously. She is believed to have great concern for the inmates of the Vicarage, next door to her tower; which is neighbourly of her. Several years ago the vicar then living there saw her several times. She takes a great interest in the affairs of the nation as well and when in 1939 the Second World War was declared, a policeman saw her standing at one of the windows of the tower. The same day she paid a visit to the Vicarage, a prey no doubt to the anxiety we all felt that day.

The Bedford Hotel is Betsy's neighbour on the other side and she makes occasional appearances there. A Scottish couple saw her moving silently round their room in her grey robe surrounded by a genteel misty light. An interesting facet of Betsy's haunting is that she never frightens anyone. Even the Scottish couple were more interested than terrified. Incidentally they had booked into the hotel fairly late and had not been informed of Betsy's existence, in the flesh or in the spirit. Indeed they had forgotten her visit until they were getting petrol in the hotel yard the next day, preparatory to driving on to Cornwall. As they waited one of them remembered the ghost's appearance and asked "Have you any ghosts around here?" .. He was quite surprised to be told that Betsy was an old inhabitant.

Many questions have been asked about Betsy and her life history. I would like to ask another. How came she to be called Betsy Grimbal? Such an un-nunlike name! Was it her own or is it an affectionate christening by the people of Tavistock?

THE COWMAN'S GHOST

There is in North Devon a valley with a stream running through it to the sea. In the valley a smaller hill rises, making a cross section pattern of a W shape, with the stream running through the bottom of the last V of the W. These contours ensure that anyone standing at the top edge of each valley can see what is happening on the slopes of the smaller hill.

It was a young farmer, standing on the eastern edge of the valley one autumn day in the nineteen sixties, who saw a figure walk down from the rough road which ran along the top of the smaller hill to examine some cattle grazing half way down the slope. The figure walked from beast to beast, carefully noting each in turn. At that moment something needed the young farmer's attention and when he looked over to the hill again the figure had vanished. There was nothing remarkable in the episode for another worker was engaged that day in weeding and burning docks only a field away from the cattle.

Not until the farmer had returned to his home on the small hill and casually described what he had seen, that he was told no one had been near the cattle for the whole of the afternoon.

Another rough laneway connected both farms and at a point in this, parallel to the place where the cattle had been grazing, the farm dogs always grew uneasy and came to heel. Normally they romped up and down this laneway quite happily. It was only at this particular place and at this particular period that they grew quiet and apprehensive. The peculiar influence on the dogs lasted for only a short time and the phantom cowman was never seen again.

MURDER AT THE SMUGGLING INN

There is an inn on the banks of the Teign at Coombe Cellars, a rebuilt smugglers haunt of a much earlier date. Some years ago a barmaid went to work there. She lived in, as it is called and was given quite a nice bedroom but for some reason she was never able to sleep comfortably in it. Every night she woke with a terrible feeling of being strangled. This went on for some time and although she complained to her fellow workers and her employer, no one took her seriously, until the latter went buying pictures one day. One of the pictures proved to be of the inn, showing the girl's bedroom where a savage murder was taking place. The murderer was portrayed in the act of strangling some unfortunate woman.

This is a fairly old story and I bring it up to date with a fresh instalment. Recently a television mechanic was engaged in fixing an aerial on the roof of the inn and was working from an attic directly over the murder room. A colleague was stationed on the landing below and things were going normally when suddenly the mechanic dropped his tools and clattered down the attic stairs. White and shaking, he refused to say what had so affected him but absolutely refused to return to the attic unless someone accompanied him. The murder room is now used as a guest room and as yet no visitor has complained of broken slumbers. It could be that the malevolent influence has transferred itself to the attic. Only the television mechanic can tell us.

COWICK BARTON FARM GHOSTS

Cowick Barton Farm, registered in Domesday Book, fell into a ruinous state and was incorporated into a new building in 1963 and opened as Cowick Barton Inn. The new building work in no way embarrasses the old inhabitants, for a phantom monk continues to make his appearance from time to time in the Inn. The same monk, or one of his old colleagues, also visits houses near the Inn and takes a saunter in broad daylight across the fields adjoining the river bank.

THE RENEGADE MONK OF LIDWELL

About two and a half miles from Dawlish going towards Exeter there used to be, in the fifteenth century, a small chapel near a holy well, the inevitable Well of Our Lady or Lady Well. The monk in charge was a bad choice by the ecclesiastic powers. He needed the support of monastic life to keep him on the straight and narrow path of holy rectitude. Left in charge of the little chapel he found the monastic diet allowed him, very little to his taste, so he turned highwayman to provide himself with a more varied and expensive diet. He was wont to wander the lonely moorland road in his habit, offering to guide travellers, and when he had assessed the profitability and possible opposition of his victim, would suddenly fall upon him and rob him. Women were enticed to his chapel for prayer meditation and rest, during which their gentle host robbed then murdered them. When his career of villainy was discovered, the holy well of Our Lady was drained and explored. It was found to be full of the bones of travellers. Most of them were the bones of women and children. Some rich travellers disappeared near Ladywell and suspicions were aroused, but the end came when the monk's judgment led him astray. He chose a homegoing sailor for a victim. When attacked, the sailor retaliated by kicking the monk into his own well.

Not unnaturally Ladywell, which in the course of time has become Lidwell, became a most haunted spot when the chapel had been allowed to fall into ruin. The monk himself is believed to haul himself to the top of the well sufficiently far to get his head and shoulder into view. He then slips back to repeat the process for the next beholder. Eerie cries and wailings from the murdered women and children waver around the remote ruins and it is a very brave person who will go near the once holy well of Our Lady at Lidwell these days.

THE GIFT BEARING GHOST OF GOODLEIGH

Nearly half a century ago two old ladies lived at Hall Cottage. They were sisters, and had lived there for many years. Goodleigh is a small parish between Barnstaple and the borders of Devon and Somerset, probably even a smaller community then than it is now so that there may have been the usual idea afloat about these two lonely old ladies, that they were witches. There is nothing in this story to suggest this possibility but there must be some reason for a villager's statement that no one would go down to Hall Cottage after dark. Which is surprising because although the intrepid pair who bought the cottage in 1970 and proceeded to make it habitable, agree that it is very extensively haunted, they have met several of the ghosts and only one was in any way disagreeable. This was a lady ghost who tried to put what felt like a weight on the wife's chest, presumably as she lay in bed for even ghosts and their antics must have some respect for the law of gravity if poltergeists can ignore it. This manifestation was resisted by the wife's willpower, which was so effective that the weight trick was never tried again.

The husband, an interior decorator and a professed atheist, a very practical character, saw the first ghost, who, in a neighbourly way, came to visit him as he stood in the caravan in which he and his wife lived before they began to renovate the cottage. This was a woman of no determinate age who was holding a glass vessel. She spoke in a soft voice, saying "I have my treasure, and you will have yours" .. before she disappeared. A few days later he found his treasure, a solid silver box, as he dug in the cottage garden. This garden seems to have attracted the ghosts for not long after the husband found his silver box, the lady of the house was pottering about in the garden with her dog when she saw a farm worker crossing the garden. She called to him, thinking he was a neighbour taking a short cut, but he instantly vanished. Her dog cowered against her and would not be comforted. All these ghosts seem harmless, generous and neighbourly. Even such heavenly bodies as they were able to influence behaved in a kindly fashion, for, when in 1970 a power cut plunged the country districts into darkness and the young couple went early to bed, a large brilliant star floated along and landed on the barn roof. As the wife watched it the star grew bigger and bigger until she woke her husband to watch it with her.

Readily it can be understood that by 1972 the various ghosts had become part of the family at Hall Cottage, but their appearance caused trouble when visitors came to stay. One of them came by car for a holiday of a few days' duration and was terrified by the sight of a tall man carrying an old fashioned lantern crossing the landing. So unnerved was he by the sight that he bolted out into the garden where his car was parked and insisted on sleeping on the back seat for the rest of his visit.

GHOSTS AT COMBE MARTIN CHURCH

A very splendid church is the parish church of Combe Martin, as befits a village with silver mines rich enough to have influenced the course of British history, for Combe Martin silver made a sizable contribution to the cost of the Hundred Years' War. The church has a magnificent tower, window tracery, battlements and bosses, and a chancel screen which once had a roodloft. It was from this screen that a parishioner saw his ghosts emerge one evening.

It was in 1920, a period not over given to ghost seeing, for a wearisome war was just over. The worshipper was not thinking of ghosts as he glanced at the screen but was surprised to see the screen door opening. Through the door came a solemn procession, a vast concourse of people, all reverently escorting a mitred bishop attended by priests, all in rich vestments, and behind them, a body of important laity, dressed in magnificent garments and carrying wands of office. Accompanying the dignitaries were yeomen, peasants and every representative of village life, in the garments of centuries past. It appeared to the amazed onlooker in the twentieth century that the occasion being re-enacted before his eyes, was some kind of dedication ceremony, for a tray was being carried before the bishop bearing a model of an important building. Silently the ghostly procession moved down the aisle and disappeared.

COMBE MARTIN'S MUSICIAN

There is said to be a ghostly violinist who plays his violin in the streets of the village. No famous concert performer he, just an itinerant musician, playing the type of music which delighted his village audiences when he was on earth. He has no special time for his playing and no special pitch. He just wanders, making his country music anywhere. A lovely ghost to have.

THE SOLDIER'S GHOST

Some years ago two schoolmistresses were conducting a party of children on a walk near the church of St. Michael on Marlpits Hill near Honiton. They were passing a thatched cottage, which has since been destroyed, and which used to stand at the side of the road, when the children saw a man wearing a long, ragged coat of a dusty brown colour, stumbling along the road towards them. He seemed quite exhausted and kept his feet with difficulty. The children bunched, frightened, as children are when such adult things as distress and want impinge upon their world, as they turned to watch the unfortunate man go by. The two mistresses, who saw nothing at all unusual, were at a loss to understand their charges' sudden silence and obvious concern so they questioned the children. They replied that they were "Looking at the funny man."

The incident so distressed the children that the mistresses made inquiries. It transpired that in 1907 a man had seen a similar apparition, dressed exactly as the children had described, at the same time and at the same place on the road. Research disclosed a sad incident in the Monmouth rebellion. One of Monmouth's men who had fought at Sedgemoor was a native of Honiton and lived at this cottage on the hill before he went to join Monmouth's forces. He was one of the few able to escape after the battle, and by moving at night and hiding by day he managed to get back to his own country. His wife and children were running to meet the weary man as he tottered towards them, when a party of troopers rode up and slashed him to pieces with their swords. The children saw the poor man's ghost just before the troopers caught him.

An interesting point for psychical researchers is the extent of the childrens' concern. Ordinary shabby men are not uncommon. One wonders if the victim's distress as he stumbled on, communicated itself to that spot on the road where his ghost appears.

A DARTMOOR GHOST STORY

This story was told to me by a rather frightened young man. He and some friends were driving in a van on Dartmoor when, in the mist which had been thickening for some time, they accidentally drove off the road. They had not gone far when they realised their error and stopped to discover exactly where they were. Peering around they thought they could see the road they had left and tried to start the engine again but nothing happened. The engine refused to start. Eventually one of them had to get out to start the engine with the handle. Suddenly, through the mist, the young man swore he saw a troop of headless horses hurtling towards him, bearing headless riders urging them on. At the same moment the recalcitrant engine burst into life. The terrified young man scrambled into the van and like maniacs they drove back to the road. Once there they lost no time returning to the safety of bright lights and the haunts of men.

Next day they remembered that in his terror the young man who started the engine had dropped the starting handle and it had been left on the moor. It was a clear bright sunny day, but they all went together to the spot in the same van. Walking on to the moor they soon found the missing handle. Round it the ground was churned up by a large number of hoof prints. None approached and none left the vicinity of the starting handle.

THE OLD REACTIONARY

Ghosts abound who centuries after their time on earth find themselves walking a couple of feet higher than they used to do, owing to the alterations of time, but this in no way perturbs them. They appear to ignore modernity. This, however, is the story of a ghost who took a positive dislike to it, and took a unique way of showing his displeasure. Instead of trying to destroy this bit of modernisation which so irritated him, he used it, all the time.

All the trouble began when it was decided to instal piped water at Denbow Farm at Farringdon near Exeter. The water was piped into the yard and was found very useful. But even when normal Devon weather prevails and water is not particularly scarce, it is not a good thing to leave taps on with water running to waste all day long. Time after time the sound of running water was heard and the tap in the yard was gushing water merrily when someone had turned it off only a minute before. This went on for some time, the farm people getting used to the exercise, until the ghost was compelled to materialise. He appeared one day in broad daylight; a short, stocky figure, standing by one of the farm buildings. He wore a cap which did not fit him too well, a shabby old black coat and trousers, with the legs tied under the knees in the old fashioned way, clothed his substantial figure and he carried an old knobby stick. No one remarked on the old fellow's presence for a while, all thinking he was waiting to see someone, when he electrified everyone by suddenly disappearing.

Inquiries were made in the neighbourhood but no one seemed

to recognise the description until a very old retired farmer in the neighbourhood identified him as an old fellow who used to work at the farm before he died many years previously.

THE FISHING BOYS' GHOST AT BRIXHAM

There are several old quarries around Brixham, many of them right on the coast, where vessels could lie close in to be laden with stone straight from the quarry floor. Access to these has become overgrown and difficult with the passing years, but the overgrown and difficult has rarely deterred small boys in search of adventure, or, as in this case, in finding a good place from which to fish. Two such small boys armed with fishing tackle were looking for such a place about thirty years ago. They were cousins, both about twelve years old, and, finding one of these abandoned quarries, scrambled down to it, picking their way over the quarry floor to sit at its edge overhanging the sea, hoping for good catches.

It was a calm day and the boys sat quietly for some time when suddenly one of them felt the hair on the back of his neck rising and prickling as a tide of fear swept over him. He felt impelled to turn and look up. There, peering over the edge of the quarry lip was a hideous yellow face, the face of a very old and very wicked man. It was the wickedness, the evil of that monstrous face which terrified the boy into immobility. There was no sign of any other part of the body, a supporting hand or arm, – just that awful face leering down at him. For some seconds the poor lad was petrified but when he could move he touched his cousin's arm and indicated the face above them, which promptly disappeared. It did not draw back. It just vanished. Both boys waited a few minutes, then bravely tackled the quarry face. No trace of anyone could be found there. No broken branches, no depressed vegetation to show where a human body had rested for those awful moments, – nothing.

No story could be discovered to account for the visitation, but so indescribably evil and malevolent was the expression on that ancient face that the small boy remembered it vividly as a grown man, he told me of that afternoon when he went fishing with his cousin twenty years before.

THE FIGHTING GHOSTS

Driving along a country road near Plymouth, a friend of mine, having driven for several hours, admits he was tired but not so exhausted that he had begun to see things which were not there. Being a keen naturalist and a lifelong countryman he was used to animals crossing the road under cover of darkness, and always drove with the possibility of having to avoid a fox, a rabbit, or even a poaching cat. But it was a couple of men, fighting like lunatics, which suddenly appeared before his front wheels. Before he could take evasive action he was in to them, feeling a slight but sickening bump as he pulled up. He almost fell out of the car, but to his astonishment there was no sight or sound of either of the combatants. One moment he was driving along with an empty road before him, next second from nowhere, the fighting pair appeared, then vanished. He walked back for some way but there was no trace of them. He walked on for some yards, still nothing. He had a passenger to consider so there was nothing for it but to continue his journey, but it was a very shaken and thoughtful man who reached home that night.

Making inquiries in various places he discovered that two men had met and fought on this particular stretch of road several years before, at the spot where he had had his vision. Both had been killed.

AFTER THE FAIR

In the early nineteenth century, country fairs were very important happenings and had been so for many a century before. Yearly sales of sheep, cattle and horses were made there and the prosperity of many a small farm depended upon the price the stock fetched at the fair.

No one knows why the man who lived on Dartmoor, between Two Bridges and Princetown acted as he did on his return from Brent Fair. He could have had bad luck there, or been cheated, or even got hopelessly drunk and was repenting at enforced leisure, but for some reason, as he rode homeward and reached the spot now known as Hangman's Pit on the road between Holne and Hexworthy, he turned aside and hanged himself on an ash tree growing there.

Waiting at home his wife was probably greatly relieved when she heard him take the pony into the stable. She heard the animal's hooves on the cobbles and listened to her husband talking to the pony as he always did. After some little time she began to wonder why he had not entered the house, and taking a lantern she went out to the stable to fetch him. There was no one there and the place was in darkness. Neither pony nor master had returned.

THE GHOST IN KING STREET

The road which Plymouth now knows as Western Approach intersects what was King Street before the Second World War, and was lined with shops before German bombs brought them down into heaps of rubble. One of these shops was a jeweller's establishment with living accommodation over it. Part of this was let off to an Irish family, including a large number of children. Almost at once this family attracted a variety of ghosts and poltergeists, making life so troublesome for them that they called in the local priest to deal with the supernatural intruders. What result was achieved by the priest was not recorded by my informant who was a descendant of the jeweller's family, but she was lyrical over the gentlemanly behaviour of their own ghost.

He appeared on summer evenings, when twilight was deepening into darkness. The family lay awake, calling to each other softly to know if each heard the faint sounds he made. The ghost was a tall seamanlike figure, who wandered the building, gazing attentively at his fellow tenants but never speaking. He seemed to have no earnest purpose in haunting the building, but could have been looking for something in a desultory way for the sounds he made, which the family heard in the summer dusk, were those any well mannered ghost would make as he carried on a little restrained rummaging.

Some years later the loft of the building was opened. It appeared to have been sealed for some considerable time and contained a number of strange objects including a bundle of peacock's feathers. These could have been the relics of old voyages taken by the ghost when he was alive and the object of his quiet searching on summer evenings.

THE CHRISTMAS GIPSY GHOST

About six or seven years ago a very tall ghost wearing a pale green hat, a long dark coat and well polished black boots and leggings, was seen walking along the road from Farway Common, near Honiton, to the inn known as The Hare and Hounds. He had been seen before, always on Christmas Eve, and he is believed to have been from one of the many gipsy families camping on the Common. What happened to him in life at Christmas time to compel him to take his walk to the inn on Christmas Eve has never been discovered.

THE MOTORING GHOST

Tiverton has many famous people in its records. Cosway, the famous miniaturist, was born there. Blundell and Greenway are famous sons of Tiverton, and a gentleman who now belongs solely to folklore, once ornamented Tiverton's intellectual society, for some years ago anyone in Devon confronted with an indissoluble problem was liable to be advised to "Go to Tiverton and ask Mr. Able!"

But it cannot be the ghost of any one of these gentlemen which haunts the drive and lodge of a large estate near the town; this is a phantom motorist, wholly modern, for he drives along in a car with a powerful engine, the noise accelerating then dying away. The sound of a car door opening then closing, the creak of a gate is heard and that is all. Except that no one has ever seen the car.

The family moving into Worth Lodge heard the ghost car soon after they took possession in 1970. A young man, a member of the family remarked that he felt a queer kind of possession about the house but had seen nothing. A lady in the family however has seen the ghost of a young man who appeared to be trying to tell her something. It may be that he will succeed in time, for the family has no intention of taking steps to rid itself of the ghost. He and his car are welcome to stay in and around Worth Lodge as long as he pleases.

THE DISAPPEARING CAR

Modbury, in years gone by, was a favourite place for those fortunate people who wished to build great houses. The Champernownes lived here and many of them lie in the thirteenth century church, with the equally important Prideaux family. Its ancient priory has disappeared but Modbury is still an interesting and beautiful place, a large number of its elegant houses still remaining into the twentieth century. Therefore it was not a great surprise to a motorist, driving from Modbury to Gara Bridge on a clear evening in the summer of 1962, when he saw an old dark blue or black Daimler approaching him round a bend in the road. So many elderly wealthy people still kept the cars of their early years. They could still afford to run them. Or perhaps some younger tourist had purchased such a car as a status symbol. Looking forward to a closer inspection he drove on. Round the bend he was amazed to find that the car had vanished. There was no lay by or side road where the old Daimler could have turned off and the grass verge was innocent of tyre marks. The old car and its occupants had disappeared completely.

A week later the same man had occasion to be on the same road at the same time and again saw the old car approaching.

This time he was able to notice that it had a primitive type of roof rack, before it vanished as before. Three times on three different occasions he saw the car before he mentioned the matter to local people, to find that it was a well known apparition. They added that the driver wore a peaked cap and a dark jacket, like an old fashioned chauffeur, but his face was never visible. No one could discover any story to account for it or its disappearance.

LEAWOOD AND ITS GHOSTS

Between Tavistock and Okehampton lies the village of Bridestow and in the treelined lane leading down from the main road to the village is the entrance to Leawood, a beautiful house set among trees, which is the home of Lieutenant Colonel Calmady Hamlyn. The house was rebuilt from the materials of a much older house and there are several ghosts in it: a daughter of the house who loved her old home very much and continues to revisit it from time to time, and a chill presence moves along the corridors at night.

A delightful old ghost is that of the family coachman in the dress of many years past, who continues to visit the store cupboard where cleaning materials are kept. He stands there with his back to passers by, choosing carefully all the things he needs before he considers it time to disappear. He has not been identified as any particular servant, but is no doubt the ghost of some old retainer of the family in days gone by.

Colonel Calmady Hamlyn's father came to Leawood as a young man with his mother and sister. His horses were his especial pride and care and he owned and raced several valuable point to point horses. The stable block is a little distance from the back of the house, and the young bachelor squire chose a bedroom in a wing of the house which was closest to the stable so that he could hear if trouble occurred among the horses at night. He had a little terrier and this dog slept on his bed. One night he awoke suddenly. His little terrier was barking angrily. Thinking that there was something amiss with the horses, the squire leaped out of bed and ran to the window, throwing it open to listen. The dog was silenced. Not a sound from the stable... then in the distance, from far away came the noise of a heavy vehicle coming down the hill, a sound which came closer and closer until he heard the vehicle, which sounded as if it might be a family coach, turn into the avenue at Leawood. It was very late and he could think of no one who could be

The stableyard at Leawood

coming to the house at that hour. By then the coach was already in the drive and was turning to enter the yard as if the way was well known to the driver. The squire leaned from the window to call to the coachman, but to his amazement nothing was to be seen as all the noise of a cumbersome coach and the clatter of shod horses passed under his window to diminish into silence at the end of the yard.

So far as is known the phenomenon had never occurred before; there is no story in the annals of the house to account for it, and, so far as Colonel Calmady Hamlyn can ascertain it has never been repeated.

THE RAILWAY GHOSTS

This is the story of some young men, all railway enthusiasts who went exploring the disused railway line from Plymouth to Launceston. Three of them are the heroes, or perhaps one should say, victims, of one story; the other young man went alone.

The three followed the line until they came to a tunnel. All had torches so they entered quite boldly. When they were some considerable way in, the torches, without warning, began to flicker, then one by one went out. Nothing they could do made any difference, the torches remained dead and they were compelled to turn and stumble their way in the darkness out of the tunnel. That three torches of different types with batteries and lamps of different ages and types could all give out together, seems impossible. News of the queer episode spread and evoked comment. Soon a grim tragedy in the history of the line came to light. At the exact spot in the line where the lights had failed a man engaged in railway maintenance had been killed.

The other young man went adventuring alone. Coming to the tunnel he entered it without a torch. The day was clear and bright and he decided that he could find his way safely by keeping close to the tunnel wall. When he was some way in, so far, that except for a greyish shadowy light reflected on the opposite wall some considerable distance on, from the end of the tunnel, he was in darkness, the ground suddenly appeared to heave beneath his feet, a movement which spread ahead, making the loose ballast rattle. He froze in horror. It was not a pleasant thought that he was sharing close confinement with something large enough to make such a stir. Nothing moved after the first disturbance. He had to get through the tunnel, for a road with a bus stop lay not far from the end of it, and that was his only way home. Quietly bending he got as close to the ground as he could and tried to see if anything bulky stood between himself and the end of the tunnel entrance light. Nothing was there. Greatly daring and no doubt nearly petrified with fright he went forward and gained the end of the tunnel in safety. That was the last time he explored that tunnel.

THE ORGANIST OF ST. JOHN'S

St. John's Church in Torquay was built in the early part of the nineteenth century and reconstructed in the mid eighteen sixties. In 1883 Henry Ditton Newman, a former pupil of the great organist, Wesley, became organist there. He became devoted to his work and to the organ and after his death, still played and practised upon it when the church was closed and locked. Many people saw him standing near the organ and one temporary organist, who could not have realised the identity of his visitor, complained angrily that he joined him at organ practice and refused to go down into the nave when asked to do so.

For some years the appearance and playing of Henry Newman became scarcer and scarcer, but in 1936 his enthusiasm burst forth once more and the church has resounded to his playing on many occasions since then. He was concerned with a scholastic establishment connected with the work of St. John's and two clergymen were convinced that they had heard his footsteps there shortly after his death.

THE LADY IN THE CORRIDOR

Hatherleigh is an attractive small town not far from Okehampton and it has a famous hotel, The George, which offers every modern facility, including a swimming pool, to its guests, although the building dates from the fourteenth century and has an old fashioned thatched roof. It was a coaching inn for many years and it is said that a phantom coach has been known to clatter up to The George on rainy winter evenings. The most remarkable ghost harboured by The George however, is the lady clad in an aura of supernatural light, who walks a corridor. A gentleman and his wife were staying at The George and had retired to their room for the night, when a gust of cold air swept into the room. So chilly did the room become that the lady thought a window had been left open and besought her husband to go out into the corridor to close it. To his amazement, the man opened the door of the bedroom to be greeted with the spectre of a woman passing down the corridor. She was surrounded by glowing light through which the details of the corridor and its furnishings could be hazily seen.

There is no known story to account for the phantom of the lady's presence in the corridor of The George, nor does she appear very often. When she does she certainly makes her presence felt for the husband and wife were almost frozen before the husband sallied forth to meet the ghost.

THE VANISHING FUNERAL

Several years ago a farmer and his wife were driving in a trap toward Roborough in mid Devon when they saw a funeral cortege approaching. The farmer drew the pony on to the side of the road and waited until the procession passed. It was a long one and the farmer and his wife exchanged comments upon its length and the time it was taking to pass as they waited. Immediately the last man passed, the farmer looked behind him to see that the procession was clear before he drove the pony back on to the road. To his amazement there was no sign of the funeral which had that minute passed them. The road was empty for as far as he could see.

THE UNIVERSITY GHOST

So many of these stories are old, but here is folklore in the making, a ghost from the age of technology. Exeter University is believed to have a ghost who walks the corridors of the reconstructed building. No information is readily available, but there is a supposition which seems to me to be impossible, even for a ghost story. I was told that the white coated individual who wanders the corridor is the ghost of an employee of a firm of construction engineers concerned in the reconstruction of the building, who was so interested in the work that he won't leave it. This is not folklore. It is a miracle.

A COTTAGE THAT WASN'T

Back in the nineteenth century when Dartmoor started becoming a fashionable place for holidays and excursions, two London ladies paid their first visit to the Chagford area. Walking on the Moor they were delighted to find a pretty cottage in exactly the surroundings they preferred. Almost any cottage would let a couple of rooms to summer visitors and the two ladies walked up the garden path, past pretty flower beds, and knocked at the door. A charming little girl answered their knock. She was dressed in white and had vivid blue eyes. She greeted the visitors politely and invited them into a sitting room, saying that she would fetch her mother. A white cat sat on a cushioned chair, and a queer black bird perched in a large cage. Both regarded the visitors with an unwinking stare, which

The George Hotel at Hatherleigh

made the ladies feel quite uncomfortable by the time the child returned with her mother. This lady, also dressed in white, spoke in a delightfully modulated voice in an accent entirely unknown to the ladies. Her clothes were good and well cut, and she wore some quite expensive jewellery. Not the kind of woman to be found in a cottage on Dartmoor in those days, however pretty and well cared for it might be.

Unfortunately the lady of the house was unable to accommodate the two ladies from London for all her rooms were taken but if they cared to come again later in the year she said, perhaps in the autumn, she would not be so busy and would be able to let them have rooms. A provisional arrangement was made for the autumn and the two departed. There was something decidedly unusual about the cottage and the inhabitants, and the two discussed the reception they had received, from the child, the woman and the pets, as they walked along. It was not until they were half way back to Chagford that they realised names had not been exchanged. They did not even know the name of the cottage or its postal address. Deciding that they could find the place again quite easily when they returned in the autumn they continued their journey and the whole affair went from their minds.

When autumn came the two went once more to Dartmoor and set off upon the moor road to find the cottage. They found landmarks they recognised as being in its immediate vicinity but no cottage. Where the neat little dwelling had stood, a pile of nettle grown rubble which had not been disturbed for years rested.

THE ESTATE AGENTS' GHOSTS

This is not the story of a repentant agent for a jerrybuilding developer, wandering for ever, waving a bunch of orders to view, it is the story of ghostly happenings vouched for by a firm of estate agents (that is, vouched for as far as any estate agent will vouch for anything) when they offered the house for sale to a transatlantic couple who were looking for a house which was genuinely haunted.

The subject of the estate agents' offer was Haldon House at Dunchideock on the hills beyond Exeter. It seems to have been rather an unfortunate house in its way, being the only remaining part of Buckingham House which was built in 1735 after the style of the Queen's House in Saint James's Park. At one time General Stringer lived there with his friend of their East India days, Sir Robert Palk. They lived in great amity, the General leaving all his money to Sir Robert's children when he died, and so moved was Sir Robert by his friend's death that he built him an impressive monument on Pen Hill. It seems improbable that their ghosts would trouble to haunt their old home, yet in 1970 the agents offered as ghost amenity, loud taps on doors and sepulchral voices calling to terrified inhabitants by their Christian names. The list also included faceless figures flitting past the glass panels of doors, but the particulars got a little confused according to the accounts available. One states that the figure is seen downstairs only. Another insists that the taps and figure appearances are confined to the first floor and occur once only in three months. However on the appearance day the ghost makes a good job of it by giving three distinct performances.

It seems that the ghosts were too much for the clients and they did not take Haldon House. The occupier in 1972 said that they had seen nothing ghostly nor had they heard the tapping. Two visitors to the house however swore that they had heard the sound of horses' hooves and heard the snapping of twigs and one saw the figure of a female servant, a ghost genuine enough for there have been few such things for many a long year in the material world.

NO WELCOME AT THE HALL

The son of Henry the Sixth's Chief Justice built the Hall at Weare Giffard and the Fortescue family lived there for many centuries. The church has a Fortescue chapel with a family tree in stone portraits on the walls. One of the memorials in the church is that of the Lord of the Manor of seven hundred years ago. His wife is there also in a wimple and crown, but oddly aloof from her lord. Now the ghost who is sometimes seen emerging from the gatehouse of the Hall and moving silently toward the church, appearing to be searching for something, is supposed to be that of Sir Walter Giffard, whose wife disappeared in Edwardian days. Have the local lorists made a mistake and is the phantom Lord of the Manor the very old lord who is searching for something or someone, the cause of the dissension between himself and the crowned and wimpled lady over seven hundred years ago? Both were Sir Walter Giffards. It might have been easy to get them muddled.

A crusader also haunted the Hall once, and a disagreeable female occasionally appeared and bade visitors 'Get you gone!' in a very peremptory fashion. It is to be hoped that she has been exorcised efficiently for the Hall is now a guesthouse and she would not be good for business.

MONEY FOR A MOTHER

One evening at Down Farm not far from Tavistock, the farmer's wife was sitting at the bedside of her sick child. The little boy was fretful and asked for water, not the water in the room but fresh cold water straight from the well. The poor mother did not care to go downstairs for water from the well as a tall and forbidding ghost was known to haunt the yard and outbuildings after dark. But the child grew more and more fretful so taking a lantern the scared woman crept downstairs.

She reached the yard in safety and was preparing to draw the water when to her horror she saw the ghost standing beside her. Quaveringly she whispered "In the name of God why dost thou trouble me?"

In a deep voice the ghost bade her draw the water for the child then follow him to a spot nearby, where she should be rewarded for her courage by a large treasure of money and valuables, if only she would dig for it. Trustingly the lady found a spade and followed the ghost. Indicating a spot where the digging should take place the ghost stood by while the lady dug, to find a treasure enough to restock the farm and provide for all her wants for many years to come. The ghost then disappeared and was seen no more.

THE CASE OF THE FRIGHTENED BRIDE

To one of the houses in a street demolished by air raids in the Second World War, a young Plymouth man brought his bride in the late nineteenth century. She was not much more than a child, barely seventeen, while the bridegroom was considerably older. I expect that like many a bridegroom he had found his wedding an expensive affair and was relieved to be offered such a good house for such a reasonable price. There seemed to be nothing wrong with it; the drains were tested and found to be satisfactory; the roof was watertight, and the walls straight and strong. Happily the young couple began housekeeping.

Then, almost immediately, began a reign of terror for the young bride and much brave front-keeping for the bridegroom, who found himself saddled with a house which was reducing his young wife to a nervous wreck and himself to a neurotic hypocrite. Each tried to keep a secret in order not to worry the other. She, the tale of the noises, the callers who hammered on the door and vanished before it could be opened, and the general atmosphere of terror which crept through the house after her husband's departure for work. He, the reputation of the house, which he had learned far too late to be of any use to either of them.

Desperately the young man tried to find other accommodation but no doubt all his capital had been sunk in the disaster house. When his wife brought him timid complaints he tried to comfort her with the usual male approach to such difficulties. "It's imagination, dear .. take no notice .." and so forth. But the terrified pair broke their reserve and clung to each other for comfort when, one evening, sitting in their cosy kitchen with a blazing fire in the range, a pair of bright and glittering human eyes scuttled over the floor and went to ground in the hearth rug, which of course harboured nothing beneath it when it was lifted. Reader, if you have been able by now to imagine a pair of glittering eyes, by themselves, scuttling over a kitchen floor, an innocent, red tiled, nineteenth century kitchen floor, you have some idea of the terror which overwhelmed the young couple. This time it was the husband who broke first. "Those eyes are my brother's" he cried "Something bad has happened to him. I know it" .. All the wife's terrors then found voice and she recounted the story of her life in her first home as a wife. The thunderous blows on the door, the gentleman on horseback who, practically every evening appeared in the street and kept watch on the door of the house, riding backward and forward. The sobbing woman on the staircase, the mysterious bells which kept up a continuous ringing through the house. The poor child had endured all this with very little complaint and must have been almost out of her mind by the time her husband managed to secure another house and take her away.

When they were safely away from the place the husband told his wife all he had learned about the house. Many years previously it had been owned by a lady who entertained gentlemen friends for profit, and it was believed that she had been done to death on the staircase by one of them. Other people had seen the irate and impatient horseman but, strangely enough, none of the little bride's neighbours had seen anything of him when discreetly questioned by the girl. The eyes, to me the most terrifying of all the alleged phenomena, were new; no one had heard of them before. As the husband had recognised them, or thought he had, as his brother's, it could be that the welter of psychic force in the house had somehow tapped the young man's mind and expressed some warning of a happening which concerned only himself.

That is one Plymouth house which the German raiders were more than welcome to destroy.

KILWORTHY GHOSTS

This is one of the famous ghost stories of Devon. History of course interferes with it, but I am going to repeat it here in the hope that there could be perhaps one reader who has not heard it before. At the same time I beg the rest of you to persevere and have patience for there are one or two bits of local colour I gathered myself and now add to the stories of Kilworthy.

Kilworthy is about two miles from Tavistock. Its gardens and grounds remain as they were to a large extent, although the house was largely rebuilt in 1800. In the sixteenth century Sir John Glanville, a judge, lived there with his wife and children, one of whom became the ghost who now haunts the house. This was a daughter who had the temerity to find herself a lover presumably without asking her father's permission. The fortunate young man followed the sea as a profession and of course was away from home for many months at a time. When the irate father discovered the affair and ordered its end, his daughter refused to give up her young man. The lover was at sea and such letters as found their way to Kilworthy from him were suppressed by Judge Glanville's order. The Judge had already decided upon a husband for his daughter, one Page, a skinflint goldsmith of Plymouth, who was looking for a young bride in order to disappoint his relatives expecting to inherit his riches.

Time went on and apparently abandoned by her absent suitor the poor girl became very depressed. Her father noted this and pressed the attractions of Mr. Page's purse and person until the unfortunate young woman gave in and became Mrs. Page. Even then, had she not taken her own maid to Plymouth with her, her ghost would not now have to haunt her old home. This woman was devoted to her young mistress and detested the old goldsmith, particularly when he dismissed his own servants and insisted that his wife and her maid between them should clean and care for his house, the matrimonial home, as well no doubt as cooking such meals as his parsimony allowed.

On this scene of misery came the young lover, home from sea. Meeting his old love one day he was horrified to see how depressed and dispirited she had become. Taxed by her for not writing to say that he was alive and well, the young man protested that he had sent many letters when and where he happened to land, and the father's despicable action in suppressing his letters came to light. Then of course, began a difficult and dangerous association, and it was not long before the maid had persuaded her young mistress to agree to a scheme for disposing somehow of the miser husband. In short, the lover, the maid and presumably the wife, between them, murdered Mr. Page.

The murder was discovered very quickly and the trio were arraigned before the girl's father. The three were condemned to death and the ghosts of at least two of them haunt Kilworthy to this day. Or so it is alleged. One, the young lover, is said to appear on the terrace. The other, the young unhappy Mistress Page, haunts the house. The most important recent appearance was made a few years ago when she came to the bedside of the Reverend John Lyon who then owned Kilworthy, and was lying in bed reading, as he awaited the home-coming of some of his household who were out on late passes, the house being then used as a school. The ghost appeared in a long grey robe and (this is important in view of the local colour to come) what appeared to impress the Reverend Lyon very much was the clarity of outline of the figure. After remaining there for a few minutes she disappeared, but the ghost has been seen on many occasions, sometimes accompanied by the rustling of silken skirts on the stairs.

Now for the local colour. When one begins to acquire a reputation for collecting ghost stories it is surprising how many one receives which never get into the ghost books. A most delightful little lady, who has since alas, died, told me the story of her early days when she was a little between maid at Kilworthy before it became a school. She was given a room at the top of the house and was terrified by the door opening slowly nearly every night. In vain did she push chairs under the knob of the door and take such defensive action as occurred to her, in the morning, more often than not, the door was wide open.

The next story brings us to the clarity of outline observation we made previously. The narrator was the daughter of another maid who also started her early career at Kilworthy. The publication in which I had recorded the information the Reverend Lyon had given me had not then been published. It was extremely unlikely that the Reverend Lyon and this lady were on ghost story swapping terms, yet the first thing told me by the daughter of the Kilworthy maid was that her mother had seen a lady, 'As plain and ordinary as you and me' .. which I thought privately could have been more tactfully expressed. A lady in grey who had walked downstairs in a perfectly natural manner, except that she disappeared before she reached the bottom. Disregarding this oddity of behaviour the young maid ran to the kitchen and asked if a visitor had gone down the front stairs, as the family were away. On being questioned she described the apparition, to be 'comforted' by the cook who informed her that she had seen the Kilworthy ghost.

A delightful if eerie story was told to me by a lady a year or so ago. I telephoned the school at Kilworthy on what I thought was the last day of term, but which turned out to be the first day of the holidays. The headmaster had already left but the lady member of the staff to whom I spoke was very encouraging when I asked permission to photograph the house. We began talking about the ghosts of the house and she told me the following story. A young American master was staying over the Christmas holidays at the school. He had his dog for company – a large red setter – and his flute. During the holiday he was sitting by the fireside practising the flute, the dog at his feet. Suddenly he felt impelled to play a strange, sad, yearning little tune which he did not know. This is to me the uncanny eerie part of the story. To play a tune at all, one must be reading music, know the tune or consciously inventing a melody. Yet this young man was playing something without knowing which note was coming next, as if something had joined his flute in becoming an instrument for something or somebody – perhaps the spirit of somebody belonging to Kilworthy, who had taken over his mental processes. The dog rose uneasily and regarded his master. As the tune ended the young man felt impelled to leave his warm fireside and go out into the hall. Dog and man went together. There was nothing there, and the heavy sense of doom and disaster which overwhelmed him as he stood there gradually faded.

THE OLD GHOST OF KINGSKERSWELL

This is a story of a ghost who appeared in a large old house near Kingskerswell, according to my informant, who added vaguely, "Or somewhere in that direction" .. but the nocturnal happenings there occurred a long time ago, when there were such things as coachmen and a plethora of maid servants. No doubt all the relatives of the old ghost are long since dead and the house itself demolished, so that there is no one now to take offence at inaccuracies.

The old gentleman whose ghost appeared to terrify his maid servants had not long died when it was ascertained that although he was believed to be very rich, very little in the way of money and valuables was to be found in the house. If the old gentleman had relatives he had no intention of benefitting them when he appeared to his three maidservants sleeping in their attic bedroom. A brilliant light surrounded the old man's apparition so that the women would have recognised him, but when he bade them rise and follow him, they were so frightened that they set up a terrible screaming, whereupon the old ghost disappeared. The noise brought the coachman running from his room, thinking the girls were being murdered. When the story of his master's appearance was related to him he jeered at their cowardice and it was arranged that he should sleep in their room the following night, while the girls occupied his.

Accordingly when the old ghost appeared to make a second attempt to persuade the maids to follow him, he found the coachman, no doubt to his great relief. When the sepulchral voice intoned 'Follow me' the coachman obediently jumped out of bed and taking a candle followed his old master. Downstairs they went, down and down until they came to an old cellar which the coachman had no idea existed. Here the ghost pointed to a blue stone set in the floor, which, he indicated, should be lifted. Underneath was a large box containing money and jewellery. The ghost signed to the coachman to remove the box and gave him to understand that it was for him. Query .. why did the ghost first try to enlist the help of the ladies? Or did the noise they make so revolt him that he transferred his benevolence to the manservant. Whatever his intention, the box provided the wherewithal to keep the coachman in comparative luxury for the rest of his life.

LADY HOWARD OF TAVISTOCK

This is the traditional story concerning the lady referred to in Tavistock and elsewhere as The Bad Lady Howard. I tell the story as it is generally known because it is a well known bit of folklore in the district, but I warn the reader that there is another story about Lady Howard in the debunking section of this book. Even in the pages devoted to ghosts I will not give any one the soubriquet of Bad unless I am sure of his or her title to it.

Having declared my interest we can proceed to the folklore history of the lady whose ghost takes so many forms. Tavistock will tell you that she had four husbands and murdered them all, and with the belligerence remaining from the first paragraph I assure you that willingly I would have helped her to murder the fourth. Be that as it may, she is believed to trundle in a coach made of bones with four skulls decorating the corner posts, all the way from Tavistock to Okehampton, accompanied by a large black hound. In other versions she is believed to have been condemned to run in the shape of a black hound to Okehampton, where she plucks a blade of grass from the Park and runs back with it to Tavistock. This she has to do until every blade of grass has been removed. Another example of the perpetual torment idea famous all over the world in folklore circles.

So hated is the memory of this unfortunate lady who subscribed to funds for the poor of Tavistock in her time, that it was believed as late as the nineteenth century, in Mary Tavy, that should anyone catch a glimpse of the coach and its passenger as it travelled the road from Tavistock to Okehampton, he or she would succumb to consumption as pulmonary tuberculosis was then called.

There is one more wholesome story of this Tavistock celebrity which is a piece of folklore in the making; a more interesting story than all the others concerning her, which have ceased fermenting as it were and are quietly gathering bouquet. The events to be related now took place about twenty years ago when a husband and wife from London were staying in Tavistock for a summer holiday. They had brought with them a large dog and it was their custom to exercise him last thing at night when he could gallop along without a lead and tire himself out before he slept. The Gatehouse, which is all that is left of Lady Howard's old home, Fitzford, has been reconstructed and stands where it always did near the junction of Callington Road and Plymouth Road. A pleasant grassy meadow stretches nearby and the dog had no doubt enjoyed a good scamper there before his master and mistress returned along the road with him, passing the Fitzford Gatehouse before turning into the Callington Road.

As they approached the building which is set back a short distance from the road, the dog romping ahead stopped suddenly, bristled, began to growl and made as if to attack something in the shadow of the Gatehouse. As a cloud swept over the moon the startled couple saw a large white stag leap from the shadow of the Gatehouse and bound away down the street. The dog, instead of leaping after it as would be expected, cowered back in terror. When the cloud passed there was no sign of any animal other than the frightened dog .. Lady Howard is believed by some to do her penance run to Okehampton every night,. by others she is said to choose St. John's Eve for it. The night the stag bounded from Fitzford Gatehouse twenty years ago, was Midsummer Eve, – St. John's Eve. Is not a white stag as attractive as a black hound?

THE WHITE BIRD OF THE OXENHAM'S

South Tawton lies high above the Taw. It has a church with an interesting and beautiful screen, and a manor which used to belong to a famous old Devon family, the Oxenham's. A John Oxenham sailed with Drake, and it was a well known story even then that before the death of any member of the family a white bird appeared. There are uncorroborated accounts of three members of the family dying about 1635 within a short time of each other and at each death the white bird made its appearance. An earlier Oxenham, a lady, died after the white bird had made its appearance, and in the eighteenth century William Oxenham, a farmer, saw the white bird in his bedroom when he was ill but not considered to be in danger of death. Nevertheless within a few days of the bird's visit he was dead.

The last days or hours of Oxenhams at places as far apart as Sidmouth, Kensington and Exeter have been marked by the appearance of the white bird, which in every recorded case seems to have entered, or tried to enter the bedroom of the dying person. The most famous, probably because it is the most romantic incident, is that of Margaret Oxenham of Oxenham Manor. She had been courted by two suitors and for some time had not been able to decide between them. Eventually she made up her mind and the wedding date was fixed. On the day before the wedding a sumptuous feast was given at the Manor. The bride's father was enjoying the festivities when to his distress he saw the white bird fluttering around his daughter's head. No one else appeared to notice anything unusual although in other reports of the white bird's visits, many people, strangers to the family, have seen the bird, and, in one case, fluttering noises were heard by strangers to the family including nurses, when the bird itself was not visible. However to return to Margaret Oxenham, it must have been an uneasy parent who conducted his daughter to the altar in South Tawton Church the following day. There are two accounts of what happened there. In one, the disappointed suitor leaped out of the congregation and stabbed the girl, afterwards killing himself. In another, the poor bride was shot. The white bird had correctly foretold the death of poor little Margaret Oxenham.

We now come to a twentieth century setting for the story of the Oxenham white bird, and another Oxenham, a lady, a Mrs. John Oxenham whose family originated at South Zeal and who died in November 1975. She had been ailing for some time and had decided finally to seek medical advice. Her daughter, who lived in London travelled to Cornwall on hearing that her mother had not been well, and stayed a night at the house of a friend on the Cornish border before going on to Cornwall where her mother lived. During her stay a large white bird, somewhat larger than a pigeon, stayed around the house, perching on the roof and windowsill. A week or so later Mrs. John Oxenham was dead.

It may be considered that the bird in this case did not visit the doomed person, but her nearest relative, but it can be remarked that Margaret Oxenham herself did not see the bird during her pre nuptial celebrations, it was her father. May not this devoted daughter, also a Margaret Oxenham, have been the subject of the legendary bird's concern? My informant in this case was the girl's friend with whom she stayed and who is an extremely sensible and responsible person. In fact a point remarkable in this history is the great pains which have been taken from time to time to substantiate the claims made by witnesses, which included people like doctors, clergy and nurses. Surely they were not all liars.

TORQUAY GHOSTS AT CASTLE-A-MARE

No collection of Devon ghost stories is complete without the narrative made famous by Beverley Nichols who took part in an investigation into the ghosts at a Torquay house some fifty years ago. A terrible story was unfolded after Mr. Nichols and two companions made their way into this deserted and semi derelict house, carrying candles, to go ghost hunting. Mr. Nichols was soon overcome by the eerie atmosphere of the place which so affected the three that after retreating to the lawn once more, one of them felt impelled to return to investigate the dark influences of evil which seemed to be emanating from a small room on the first floor. He was away for some little time when the two young men waiting outside heard noises as of a savage fracas going on in the house. They leaped to their feet and made their way to a downstairs window through which they had made their first entrance to the house, in time to receive their comrade as he literally fell out of it into their arms, pale, bruised and almost hysterical.

When he had somewhat recovered he told them that a dark shape had rushed at him and tried to knock him downstairs. After a furious struggle he managed to break away and rejoin his companions.

Naturally, exhaustive inquiries were made after these frightening happenings and eventually they learned the story of the deserted house. Many years previously a doctor lived there who either accepted patients with mental instability for treatment and rest, or had a friend in such need to stay with him. One day the patient completely lost control and killed the doctor. He then attacked the young maid servant who evaded him as long as she could but was caught and murdered as well. After these tragic events the house was empty for some considerable time and when fresh tenants came to it, it was found that the house was very badly haunted. Doors opened of themselves. Door handles were seen to turn; the doors opened long enough and far enough to allow someone unseen to enter a room, then they were closed. Ladies in velvet dresses passed up and down the stairs and running steps were heard in the corridors. No dog could be induced to enter the house and horses could only be persuaded into the stable by backing them into it.

The murders, or at least that of the doctor, was done in a small room which was afterwards turned into a bathroom and it was from this bathroom that the enormous dark force swept out which attacked the young man. Attempts were made to renovate the house for habitation but the horrors remained. This is regarded as one of the most horrible of Devon ghost stories.

THE GHOSTS OF DARTINGTON HALL

The Countess's Room at Dartington Hall near Totnes, formerly the home of the ancient Devon family of Champernowne was the chief theatre of hauntings, the lady responsible being Lady Montgomerie, who, centuries previously had lived for three years at the Hall. The White Lady was a ghost who appeared when any of the family was in danger of dying. Before the house was sold, a part of it including the front of the house was let to friends and one of their maids was closing the front door of the house one summer night when the ghost of the White Lady appeared, moving across the lawn and frightening the young maid out of her wits. Three weeks later the rector of Dartington, a member of the family, died. It seems that the ghosts warning is fixed for three weeks before a death for the White Lady also appeared exactly three weeks before one of the sons of the house died in 1897.

A lady member of the family was sitting up late one evening in the Countess's Room, when she heard sounds as of footsteps overhead in a room which was being used as a nursery. Thinking the footsteps were those of a young nursemaid she made a mental note to suggest to the head nurse that the young maid should not be up and about so late. Next day she went to the nursery with this end in view, but before she could make the suggestion the head nurse begged that her mistress would be kind enough to speak to the young nursemaid when she went into the nursery again at night as the girl was rather nervous. Her mistress's obvious surprise provoked further discussion and it appeared that a lady had entered the night nursery, walked across the room and burnt a piece of paper in the dying fire. It was her footsteps the mistress had heard the previous day as she sat in the Countess's Room.

Another lady member of the family used to assert that an old lady was in the habit of entering her room at night, leaning over her bed and gazing into her face. The drive near the river also was haunted, a headless horseman riding through the gate and up the drive. A more pleasant ghost used to play the piano at Dartington Hall, for one day one of the Champernowne ladies heard a beautiful piano solo being played in the room overhead. When she ran up to congratulate the pianist she found the room locked and everything silent. This lady's mother was an excellent pianist and when one day the young lady heard deep sonorous chords being played on the piano in the room above, she went to tell her mother about it. The older lady remarked at the coincidence; her own mother had heard such chords being played in the same way.

The Hall now belongs to strangers to the Champernowne family, but before the sale was completed a queer incident took place. The Steward's room on the tower stairs was the place where the estate accounts were always kept and when most of the family's effects had been removed a member of the family paid a last visit to the tower and the steward's room. Here he found the floor strewn with accounts relating to eighteenth century transactions of the family. These he gathered up and replaced in the pigeonholes lining the room. When the matter was mentioned to the rector he was astonished. A short time previously he also had ascended to the Steward's room, found the floor littered with the same accounts and restored them to their place in the pigeonholes.

All that followeth is folklore ------

LUCK CEREMONIAL

Even today superstition concerns itself with practically every human activity. Domestic affairs attract most of the taboos and the old farmhouses and cottages of the Devon countryside are famous places for meeting them. It was in an old thatched cottage near Honiton that I was taught how to cope with what used to be called 'a pair of bellows' – those things shaped like the ace of spades with a kind of short pipe at the working end, with which people used to encourage their fires to burn. These should never be lent or borrowed, and even when kept at home a certain amount of care should be exercised in dealing with them. Never allow them to rest nozzle upward, and on no account place them on a table.

If you are lucky enough to have an open coal fire in a grate with bars, you may see a scrap of dull black substance hanging from one of them. Scientists may call it carbon, but in Devon it is called a stranger, and vigorous hand clapping close to the bars will dislodge him. Start counting from the day's date and the number of claps required to get rid of the stranger will give you the day of his coming. If the fire burns brightly there will be a frost that night, and if the fire is dull and slow burning a long steel poker set on end, point upward against the top bar will help matters. It keeps away the witch who is overlooking the fire.

Should your ears burn you can be sure someone is talking about you. If the left ear burns you are being praised, if the right, then scandal is being retailed. If both burn your friends are numerous and busy. Should a knife be dropped, a visitor will call that day; the person nearest the knife is the person for whom the visitor will be calling. Tables seem to signify a great deal in the world of prophecy. Not only bellows but boots, shoes and slippers should be kept off them, and housewives cooking oven-to-table dishes should beware, any cooking vessel on a table will cause a quarrel.

Always eat a mackerel from tail to head; and while discussing directional luckbringers, be sure to turn your mattress from bottom to top instead of from side to side, because 'Turn your mattress from foot to head you'll never need to beg your bread.' Also if you leave your house to go upon a journey, then find you have to return to it for something you have forgotten or for some other reason, always sit down for a while, or perform some small task, then make a fresh start.

You will appear to have completed one journey, returned, and set out upon another. It may make the bad luck you have been risking, a little better, but the malevolent spirits overseeing such affairs are a suspicious lot and may not be taken in. Also when on the way up or down stairs, never turn. I was not told what happens if this advice is disregarded but it is sure to be something nasty.

Around the house and garden keep a careful watch for ants. In the west country these little creatures are believed to be a race of tiny elves in process of diminishing out of existence, but they are still capable of bringing bad luck to anyone destroying a colony of them.

What now follows can be called the Dolour of May. There are more dire warnings, taboos and do's and don'ts about this beautiful month than about any other period in the calendar. And rejoice with me for I have found, if not the reason, a possible source of this calumny on the merry merry month of May, but this we will keep until the tale of woe is ended, and begin with a warning about blankets. These should never be washed until May is over. Washing blankets in May washes away the life of one of your family, or, some say, the head of the family. Not only blankets but clothes need careful consideration in May for we have all heard that it is inadvisable to cast a clout till May be out. And even if we avoid all the foregoing perilous activities and the weather happens to turn warm we may still be in trouble, for a warm May means fat churchyard hay; a dismal consequence of the observation that 'March will search, April will try, but May will prove if you live or die.' Whitewashing should not be done in May for the whitewasher risks washing away his own life. Brooms, brushes or besoms bought in May wear out quicker than those bought in any other month; and if you happen to be a kitten try not to be born in May, in Devon at any rate, for you are practically certain to be drowned. All in all, the safest thing to do in May is to sit quietly in a corner and wait for the first of June.

As I remarked at the beginning of this diatribe on May; all this foreboding about one month in the twelve to the exclusion of the others, set me wondering and I decided that at some time in the future I would try to find the reason for all this May misery. But enlightenment was at that moment awaiting me for almost at once I found, entirely accidentally, a convincing solution in a casual reading of Sir Thomas Browne's 'Letter to a Friend,' published with his Religio Medici. In this he comments that the intimate friend they both mourned "Lived not until the middle of May and confirmed the observation of Hippocrates of that mortal time of the year when the leaves of the Fig Tree resemble a Daw's Claw!" ... So we can blame this ancient Greek doctor for all the doom and disaster in May ideas. Incidentally I am informed by an assurance executive that November is the popular month for dying these days, what ever happened in ancient Greece.

But things aren't always lucky even in January, for if you pay a bill or any sum of money away, on the first day of that month you will find yourself paying out money for the rest of the year.

Now here is some advice for the farmer and his household. Never let a kettle boil dry, your cows will go dry as well. Then take care to get all the necessary knife sharpening done by Saturday evening. 'If you sharpen a knife on Sunday, you will have to skin on Monday.' Perhaps you may feel that some evilly disposed person has 'overlooked' your farm. If so, the only thing to do is to find a large copper or brass pan, shaped like a milk pan. This you half fill with cow dung (for your sake I hope this takes place in winter) which must be fresh from the cow sheds. Balance it on your head and walk over the fields with it. You will, no doubt, prefer to endure the 'overlooking'! Then let us take buttermaking. There are so many folk lore ideas about butter making that a book could be written on that subject alone, but let us presume that all the pitfalls have been avoided and the butter is made, and a pat of it lies before us. Never cut it from both ends. It is very unlucky, as well as untidy.

The next piece of advice may be considered archaic, but who knows what will happen if tractors and oil get much dearer, and all the heavy horses are eaten. In that case we shall have to return to oxen and we must beware of working them on Good Friday, for on that day they are liable to drop dead in the yoke. Still in the world of agriculture, the sheep farmer should remember that the first lamb of the season, like a Victorian child, should be seen and not heard. Unlike the child, when it has been seen once it can bleat its head off if it likes. When first noticed it should be looking straight into the shepherd's face, in which case he and the flock will be lucky for the rest of the year.

Not long after the first lamb is seen, the cuckoo will be

heard. Take note of your occupation when you hear him for the first time, for that is what you will be doing for the rest of that year. Should you be unmarried and be standing on grass when his double note is heard first, you will be married before the year is out. Devonians assert that Poughill Church keeps a box of cuckoos in the tower. They are let out every April so that they can go to Witheridge Fair.

Our next piece of lucklore concerns feathers and I am delighted to discover that I unconsciously have followed this bit of ceremonial all my life without realising it. If a feather is seen lying on the ground it should be picked up and pushed quill first into the ground. This is a great luck bringer. All my life I have 'planted' such feathers when I found them, but only because I felt that such beautiful things should not be left to be trodden upon and spoilt. The idea has a factual basis for when arrows were so treated they were safe.

Finally for all of us engaged in odd jobs around the house; it is unlucky to do any of the following: Pour medicine back into its bottle, it reverses the cure. Knit on a Sunday. Keep pot plants in a bedroom or a peeled onion anywhere in the house. Lose or break a wedding ring, pick flowers from a churchyard or cemetery, or watch a friend quite out of sight after saying farewell to him.

All the foregoing items of luck lore are innocent and some even pleasant. Here is one old Devon custom for bringing luck which, I hope, has disappeared and never will be resuscitated. In the nineteenth century, and probably for centuries before, the Devon countryman set off after the first butterfly of the year and hunted it from bush to bush, over hill and dale until he caught and killed it. This bit of savagery was considered to bring good luck for the rest of the year. How much nicer would it have been to rely upon the benevolent ash tree, for its leaves would appear about the same time as the first butterfly, if one does not count the odd wandering brimstone. No running and scrambling would be necessary, all that was needful was to pick an ashleaf, murmuring the while 'Even ash I thee do pluck, hoping thus to gain good luck'.

SPELLS AND CURES AND THE LIKE

Although the admiration expressed hereafter for the art of natural healing and its Devon practitioners, is perfectly genuine, it must be confessed that undertaking most of these cures is not advised. For instance I regret that owing to the abolition of capital punishment it will not be easy for anyone to experiment with the following cure for scrofula which comes from North Devon, but for the very determined person there is always the museum at Scotland Yard. To cure scrofula, then, obtain a hangman's rope and strike the patient with it, where, is not stated, neither the number of blows required. The rope is then coiled up and placed in a canvas bag and hung round the patient's neck. He carries it until he is cured.

Corns are more frequent problems and entirely to be rid of them they should be pared on a Friday, when the moon is quartered. Saturday will do if the victim is desperate, but Friday is the ideal day.

In the event of an adder biting a farm animal, the farmer should say the following verse over it:

Adder, adder, adder, Lay under a stone,
He hath done this creature a wrong,
One fold, two fold, three fold,
In the name of the Father and the Son and the Holy Ghost, Amen.
Let this sting go away if the Lord God please. Amen.

To cure human ills the procedure is much the same. These Biblical cures are common all over Britain. The charms were usually written on scraps of paper and obtained from the local wise woman or man. They generally begin with a little preamble before the serious business of the cure is undertaken. The hero or heroine of the story is a saint, or the Virgin Mary or Christ. The hero meets with the patient as he sits suffering by the roadside and inquires what ails him. The patient names his trouble. In a suitable verse the hero bids the demon causing the patient's suffering to depart. In the north of Scotland these verses are inscribed on scraps of paper which are greatly treasured and known as 'lines'. In that part of the world many cures for wasting diseases in cattle, and mastitis in milking herds were 'cured' by similar charms. The wise men or women were treated with great respect and not a little fear and their services were in great demand. The same system for apprenticeships for orphans which was in practice in Devon until comparatively recently, also obtained in the north of Scotland, and although there is no recorded evidence that they were treated badly, there existed in farming households what can only be described as degrees of solicitude. There is a story that a farmer with a very good herd of cows called in a local wise man when one of them sickened.

After an examination and much ceremonial the wise man looked grave. Calling the farmer aside he confessed that the case was a bad one and likely to prove fatal. He could not get rid of the trouble entirely, but had the farmer a young orphan farm servant whose services could be dispensed with, for it would be easy to transfer the disease!

Not so commercially minded was an old wise woman in Devon who met a distraught mother carrying her badly scalded child. At the inquest on the child she stated that she 'charmed' the child there and then on the road, by repeating to herself 'There were two angels coming from the north. One brought fire, the other frost. Out fire, in frost, in the name of the Father In the name of the Son in the name of the Holy Ghost.' This was good for scald, but the charm would only work if used by a man for a woman or a woman for a man. Woman to woman. 'Twant do no good' ...

From a kindly old Devonian of the nineteenth century let us go to an up to date story of charming, which is just at second hand and no more for this story was told to me by one of the principals. About two years ago my friend who was a Queen Alexandra's nurse of considerable experience, tried to deal with two large veruccas on her daughter's foot. She took appropriate measures but the growths were obdurate, so she took the girl to a doctor. Treatment followed, still the growths remained. By then the girl's fiance was growing worried. A staunch Devonian he bravely suggested consulting a wart charmer. Now this is rather like offering a copy of 'Everyman His Own Lawyer' to a Q.C., but this young man had his way and telephoned a well known wart charmer, a lady, asking when he could bring the girl over to see her. To his surprise he was told that no visit was necessary, just the number of veruccas and the girl's name. These he gave. Next day, as the dressing from the girl's foot was removed, the two growths fell out with it. An amusing part of the story is that the mother would not admit the wart curer's part in the affair to the doctor.

An essential part of long distance wart curing seems to be the accurate description and number of the growths. There is a story that a young man being troubled with a number of warts, counted them and reported the number to his wart curing consultant. To the amazement of both the warts remained untouched and showed no sign of disappearing. Piqued no doubt by this professional unco-operation, the wart curer inquired if the young man had counted his warts correctly. He counted them again. He had missed one. The new total was reported and in due course all the warts disappeared. Some wart curers 'buy' the warts for a small coin which has to be thrown away, and a heart warming belief obtains that no charge must be made for the service, although at present at some celebration date such as Easter or Christmas is rarely refused.

Cures, charms and luckbringers, all have a share in the benevolence of the ash tree, surely the most important tree the countryman can grow. Some of its folklore history and details of its uses are in the section about plant life; here is set forth a famous old Devon cure for a child with a hernia or one that does not seem to thrive. The parents seek a young ash tree and when they find it they slit the trunk vertically. Wedging the trunk open they take the naked baby and standing one on each side of the tree, they pass the child backward and forward headfirst through the gap, three times. The trunk is then bound together so that not the tiniest gap remains. As the tree grows together so do the tissues of the ruptured child. The sickly child undergoes further treatment. For three mornings after the ceremony, early morning dew was collected from the same tree and the child bathed with it.

At the season of the year when the snake sloughs off its old skin, the Devon countryman kept a sharp eye upon low growth where the snake had rubbed its irritating old skin away. This dead snakeskin was treasured by hedgers for the relief of thorn injuries. If a thorn was imbedded in the flesh so firmly that it could not be extracted by ordinary methods, the discarded snakeskin was bound upon that part of the hand farthest away from the thorn. The idea being presumably that the thorn would retreat from that emblem of primeval devilry, a serpent, and in doing so remove itself from the patient's flesh.

In the nineteenth century Holsworthy Church was the scene for an old cure for fits. On a Sunday afternoon a young girl appeared at church escorted by thirty young men. After the service the girl left the church and took a seat in the porch. As each young man came out of church and passed the girl, he dropped a penny into her lap, the last man taking the twenty nine pennies and leaving a half-crown. Taking the silver coin in her hand the girl re-entered the church and walked three times round the communion table holding the half-crown in her hand before her. Afterwards she had the half crown made into a silver ring which she believed would cure her of her complaint. At one time, about the eighteenth century, cramp rings were made and worn, a practice which is not unlike the modern idea of wearing copper for easing the pains of rheumatism.

Donkeys were always to be found somewhere in a Devon village in years gone by and they were found useful when children fell ill. Should a little girl catch scarlet fever a male donkey was found and she was passed, well wrapped up it is to be hoped, under the belly of the donkey and over its back three times. For a boy so afflicted a jenny donkey had to be looked for.

Whooping cough entailed a rather nastier cure. Seven hairs were drawn from the dark cross on a donkey's withers. These were placed between two slices of bread and butter and the poor child was induced to eat the sandwich. If sheep were more plentiful than donkeys, the little sufferer from whooping cough was taken among a flock of sheep and held under the animals' noses in the hope that one or two of them would sneeze or cough over the child. If that procedure was too time consuming, the next best thing was to take the child to a sheep fold and wait until one of the sheep decided to rise from her sleeping position. The child was then placed in the warm hollow, and after that I suppose no one worried about the whooping cough, the poor little soul had double pneumonia!

PLANTS IN FOLKLORE OF DEVON

The study of plant life in connection with folklore is an enormous field. Mandrake, drawn screaming from the earth at midnight, the fatal nightshade; vervain, looking much more ominous when written than the verbena it is; these and hundreds more have been used in Britain for spells and magic, witchcraft and divination, for centuries. All that can be done here is to mention Devon's usage of a few of such plants; its trees and its 'arbs' – a word which will be heard in conversation for a long time before it is realised that herbs are being discussed. Sometimes one is awed by a word which, after patient investigation, links present day Devon with ancient beliefs and cultures, as on the occasion I became interested in a plant which I could not identify from description or use. Only the mention of an alternative name 'mandrigger' told me that a corruption of mandragora, the mandrake, was meant, and momentarily transported me to an older quieter world, if one not less evil, where my old friend's mandrigger or 'devil's apple' was known, grown and feared.

Then there is garlic. Not far from Plymouth there is an old churchyard surrounded by this plant, or was a year or so ago when I visited it. A villager here and there will, if he approves of you, admit that garlic was planted in the old days around the church, to keep whatever undead person may chance to be buried there from wandering beyond the confines of the burial ground to assail the villagers. This too is a world wide belief in the power of a plant. In fact in the following references to plants with Devon use in folklore, it has to be admitted that practically all of them share their use with other counties and even other countries. Devon's special tree, the apple shares the oldest myth in the western world, the Garden of Eden but a start must be made somewhere and we will begin with the apple.

Apple

Devon being a great cider county, apple orchards have been plentiful there for many a long year. The Devon growers included their trees in the year's ceremonies, and when Christmas came along they did not forget the apple trees which provided them with the cider to be drunk in great quantities at this festive time. Nearly all the fruit growing districts in Britain have a history of fertility-inducing customs but I like to think that although the west country farmers might have realised that they were obeying the laws of their old religion when they wassailed the apple trees, they went into the dark orchard in a friendly spirit, including the old trees in the family celebrations and merrymaking so to speak. Orchards were among the first efforts of man when he became interested in agriculture and these rites for inducing a good crop are very old indeed.

When the Devon farmer went out wassailing the apple trees he, or his women folk, had already put in a fair amount of preparation. First a large pan of spiced ale was placed before the fire and a string of apples arranged above it to roast so that as each apple became soft and cooked it fell off the string into the pan of ale. The resultant toddy was known as Lambswool and when ready was carried out into the orchard, where each tree was wassailed in turn. On Twelfth Night a large milkpan of cider containing fragments of baked apple was taken into the orchard and placed as near the centre of it as possible. The owner and his family and servants would gather round each armed with a large earthenware mug. A mugful of the cider was dipped out by each person and carried to an apple tree, part of the contents being drunk to the health of the tree. The following verse in one variation or another was recited: "Here's health to the good old apple tree, well to bear in pocketfulls, hatfulls, and good bushel bagfulls." The remainder of the mug's contents was then thrown against the trunk. If the ceremony is not carried out many farmers assert that the tree will not bear fruit the following season. Presumably the scene in the orchards was lighted by lanterns or perhaps a bonfire and the spectacle of merrymakers roaming from tree to tree splashing cider over the trunks must have been a delightful one.

In other parts of Devon and in Somerset a different rite is performed. Here the farmer takes his gun and goes into his orchard in daylight, "to shoot the Devil out of the trees". The idea at the bottom of this rite is, no doubt, the rough pruning the peppering of shot provides.

When the tree has borne its fruit the apples also take a place in rural folklore. Children as far from Devon as the North of Scotland expect to get an apple on All Hallowe'en and apples were used for many amusements at that time. A fascinating ploy for the young of both sexes was the business of consulting apple peel to discover the name of one's future life partner. To do this an apple was peeled carefully so that the skin formed one long piece. This was swung once round the head and tossed over the left shoulder. The pattern made by the peel as it lay on the ground was studied carefully. The initial of the future bride or groom could be discerned according to the enthusiasm brought to the exercise.

The fortunes of the family could also be told by studying the tree during the year. If, in the autumn, an apple tree bears mature apples as well as a blossom, someone in the family will die before the year is out.

The few small apples left on the trees after the crop has been gathered was the perquisite of the farm's population of pixies. This residue was known as the Pixie whord, or Pixie Worting, and disappeared as the autumn gave way to winter. I think the blackbirds helped the pixies.

The Ashen Faggot

This important survival of the old Norse mythology in a twentieth century version, appears on our Christmas cards; even, chocolate coated and ornamented with an artificial robin on an artificial holly spray, as a Christmas cake, but however it masquerades in a British winter, the Ashen Faggot is no symbol of Christian Yuletide but a relic of the old religion of the men from the north. Herrick, the townsman turned country vicar, celebrating his Christmases at Dean Prior knew all about the Ashen Faggot and the ritual attached to it, for in one of his less happy verses he writes:

Come bring with a noise, my merry merry boys,
The Christmas log to the firing.
While my good dame she,
Bids ye all be free,
And drink to your hearts' desiring
With the last year's brand
Light the new block and
For good success in his spending
On your psaltries play
That sweet luck may
Come while the log is a-tending.

The Ashen Faggot was cut in most Devon farmhouses only a few hours before it was to be burned, for 'Ash dry or Ash green makes a fire fit for a queen', A substantial piece of ash wood was the centre piece of the Faggot, sometimes even a small ash trunk. Hazel and other tree branches were bound to it by hazel withes, usually four, to represent the four seasons, although some Devonians used as many as possible. As each bond burned through and released blazing branches a fresh measure of cider was brought into circulation. While the Ashen Faggot burned, all social differences were forgotten and master and man, mistress and maid ate drank and made merry.

In some old farmhouses the youngest child of the family was placed upon the Ashen Faggot as fire was put to it, and upon his resultant behaviour his stamina and future success in life was assessed. The poor infant was probably terrified but if he or she remained still without showing fear until removed by his elders, his future integrity and prosperity was assured. This is a relic of the old Norse ordeal by fire brought to Devon firesides, and even when the festival was over the charred remains of the Faggot were disposed with due tribute to the Fire God of the north for it was placed outside with the charred end uppermost so that the god could see that due tribute had been paid to him. Of course it was only commonsense to leave a log which could still harbour a spark or two, outside until it could be considered quite safe. When this was decided the Faggot remains, as Herrick commented, were stored carefully until the following Christmas when they were used to start that year's Ashen Faggot on its way.

So successfully had the custom of burning a log from the Tree of Life at the festival of the turning of the year established itself in Christian Devon, that when in the late nineteenth century, a survey was made in the South Devon area it was discovered that in one postal district alone, thirty two farmhouses and cottages burned their Ashen Faggot at Christmas.

Ash

The Danes assailed Devon from both coasts. They landed on the North coast afresh from successes in Wales to come to grief at the hands of Alfred's army. They landed on the South coast at several points for the story runs that the red cliffs of the western part of the South Coast of Devon are red for ever with the Danish blood which was spilt there. Also they sailed up the Dart to harass the villages under Dartmoor. With all this invasion it was inevitable that Danes settled in many parts of Devon and brought their beliefs in the magic of their sacred tree, Ygdrasil with them. Ygdrasil, or Yggdrasil as it is also spelt, has been identified as the Ash. It is the mystic Tree of Life of the Norsemen. For them it typifies the whole of existence. Its symbolic three roots stretch to gather in the realms of the gods, of the giants and of death; its trunk holds up the earth; its boughs canopy the world and reach beyond the skies. Ygdrasil endures.

The Norsemen say that Odin fashioned the first man out of ashwood and many babies in old Devon were given a first feed of ash sap exactly as a young Viking was introduced to sustenance centuries before. The ashes from a fire of ashwood were believed to cure leprosy and, with the hazel, its twigs bound into a wreath and hung about the neck of an animal preserves it from harm, particularly from witchcraft. The very young leaves of a budding ash were used as a healing application for skin disorders and the tree itself was used for the cure of almost every ailment of the young.

Beech

The Beech has a lovely silken grey bark which is ideal for the carving of initials, usually inside hearts, and many a Devon beech bears such devices sometimes with dates many years past, carved beneath them. The tree has not, so far as I can discover, much of a place in folklore in Devon, but the old beech tree which used to stand near the ruined Castle of Berry Pomeroy used to be known as a Wishing Tree. There were two procedures to follow, in one the postulant knelt close to the tree and whispered his wish with his lips close against the trunk. In the other he walked backward round the tree three times while the wish was being made. It is a curious fact that a grey smooth barked tree in Indian forests used to be known as a Wishing Tree.

Blackthorn

This tree or bush has a bad reputation. It is said to spring from the blood of murder and it attracts witches. All I can offer from my own knowledge is that its tart little damsonlike fruits make good sloe gin.

Bramble

Was used with Dock and Nettle leaves as a complement to a charm for scalding. A bramble shoot with the tip rooted a fair way from the parent bush was a useful piece of therapy for rheumatic sufferers. The poor souls had to crawl beneath the arched branch. Useful for rheumatic dwarfs. Bramble was also used in water to give second sight, or 'open eyes' as my informant put it, and the decoction taken warm at night cured depression from love troubles. A versatile plant indeed.

Elder

This is a famous folklore tree in Devon as elsewhere. Planted by a house or gate it preserves the inhabitants from the evil effects of witchcraft. It was one of the trees which was supposed to have been used for the Cross and an old hedger, if you can find one, will tell you that you should ask the elder's pardon before cutting it when trimming a hedge. I offer the practical suggestion that if cursed with it in a hedge, for it makes an open and branchy place, the elder should be cut a little lower than the rest of the hedge. It looks odd for a while but elder grows so quickly that long before the hedge needs cutting again it will be level.

Wherever Dwarf Elder grows in Devon it is said that Danish blood was spilt, and a group of such trees is believed to denote a Danish battlefield.

Hawthorn

Is a tree beloved of the Little People and sacred in ancient Greece. It was used a great deal in magical ceremonies, but when in blossom is said to have a bad reputation. It should never be brought into the house, however attractive the beautiful flowers may be. In some parts of Devon it can be used for house decoration quite safely after the first day of May, but until then the fairy people like it kept outside.

There is a belief that the elves plant hawthorn, and if the trees are uprooted without due apologies to the King of the Elves, the thorns from the trees will stab the uprooter all night. I had this story from a charming old gentleman who had done much hedging in his day and who swore that when he had uprooted a lot of young thorns in a field, forgetting to ask the pardon of the Elf King, he couldn't sleep for the 'stabbing in my legs'. Tentatively I suggested night cramp, a disability of advancing years, but he would have none of it.

A wonderful story about a famous thorn comes from Somerset, and if purists complain that the Glastonbury Thorn is at Glastonbury and the events which gave it that name took place there, I reply that there is a young offshoot of the Glastonbury Thorn in the churchyard of St. Eustachius, the Abbey Church of Tavistock. Briefly the story runs that Joseph of Arimathea found himself in Britain and wandering in Somerset he thrust his staff into the ground at Wirral Hill, where it immediately took root and burst into full bloom. A piece of the Glastonbury Thorn was taken to Tavistock where it has flourished. Whether Glastonbury claims the parent tree to be that staff Joseph planted I do not know, the provenance of that is surely Glastonbury's affair. All I can say is that I have visited Tavistock's little tree every Christmas for three years and have never yet seen a blossom on it, although the Glastonbury Thorn is said to burst into bloom on Christmas Eve. We must conclude that the plant prefers Somerset to Devon.

Hazel

Is a very powerful tree. Used with ash it is still more powerful, the two trees being used together increasing the power as two drugs are used in medicine. Twined together round the neck of an animal it preserves it from witchcraft, adder bite and almost every other ill known to beast.

A hazel wand is used in occult ceremonies and a Y shaped twig or branch is used in water divining. About forty years ago an old gipsy diviner showed me how to cut and use a hazel dowsing twig. This was his method. Find a strong twig which branches as equally as possible into a Y shape. Cut the twig a few inches below the junction, leaving the two branches fairly long. Cut these off equally, leaving a capital Y shape with longish arms. Take the ends of the two branches, one in each hand, laying them across the hand from the outside of the palm to the hollow above the thumb, which is placed over the cut end of each branch. Then go looking for water. The short stem should bend downwards and vibrate if over a hidden spring or other water. If the reader finds he is a natural diviner he should practise the art. It disappears with disuse.

Lilac

Lilac should not be brought into the house however sweetly smelling and beautiful the great heads of blossom may be. It brings bad luck with it. In some parts of the county lilac used to be called may, which is another name for hawthorn and it could be that the two trees have become confused. Personally I risk disaster if I am lucky enough to be given lilac.

Mountain Ash

Another very powerful plant which is used in witchcraft; also in the early ecumenical days of Christianity and the old religion it was carried in procession in early church ceremonies. A strong protection against evil, it was also used as a confirming or emphasising agent in spellbinding. A very beautiful little tree but one to be treated with reserve and respect.

Herbs and Flowers

Among the herbs and flowers are several which have spell-binding properties and that charming little chickweed, the stitchwort, springs to mind. It stars the Devon hedges with the red campion and the bluebell in early spring making an unforgettable floral pattern for the wayfarer travelling slowly enough to perceive and enjoy it. But even if you stop to pick campion or bluebell, it is advisable to leave the stitchwort where it is. It is beloved of the pixies and they are worse than conservationists when annoyed.

Perhaps you have a plant of the lemon verbena getting past its prime and you think it is time to take some cuttings from it. Find a married lady, or one with matrimonial prospects in near view to do your gardening for you. Lemon verbena cuttings never fail to strike if such a lady sets them.

Verbena is one of the many plants with protective powers against witchcraft and all illwishing, and garlic was known as a safeguard against vampires and such creatures in Devon before Bram Stoker wrote his famous book, although vampires do not appear often in Devon stories.

Parsley is a plant with two opposing opinions. In some parts of Devon it is prepared to thrive if the lady of the house is the dominant character; in other parts it prefers male domination. To be sure of a crop it would seem wisest to have parsley grown by bachelors and spinsters, each with separate establishments.

Heart's Ease, the little Viola tricolour, with its tiny yellow and purple petals is a famous consoler of maidens suffering from the pangs of unrequited love. It should be gathered on St. John's Eve and presented to the errant swain, surreptitiously if necessary.

Hypericum in all its varieties has many uses in folklore, magic and healing; one of its shrub members being known in Devon as a universal healer for any kind of wound. Another perennial hypericum is used in 'eye opening' ceremonial and the same plant has its place in Midsummer celebrations.

PIXIES AND PIXIE LEADING

The Devon pixie is an amiable little body, taking him all the way round. He is bribed with milk if assistance in household tasks is required of him, although sadly these days people prefer buttons and switches and gadgets of every description. Pixies can be mischievous little people though, and are given to misleading people. There is a well known story of a family in a field near Ashburton who, in broad daylight, with the church-tower in the distance as a bearing, still could not find their way out of a field which they knew to have four gates. One of them suddenly remembered an old story and took off his coat, turned it inside out and replaced it on his shoulders. The gate then suddenly appeared beside them.

A dark night is not the best time for finding one's way out of a field even if the field belongs to you and you are very familiar with it. A friend of mine helps her husband at lambing time and was engaged with a lamb and its mother when for some reason her husband had to return to the farmbuildings, leaving her to return with the lantern when her task was completed. Before he went he pointed out the gate dimly seen in the rays of the lantern. But when she was ready to leave the field my friend could not find that gate although she had not moved the lantern. She crept round and round the hedges but was still in the field when her worried husband returned to look for her.

Pixies do not always confuse people. My own adventure could be regarded as a case of benevolent pixie activity. I was trying to find a rough stoned pathway across a heathery moor on a dark night. Several times I found myself on grass and, enticed by a glimmering of greying light to the left, I moved toward it downhill, only to find myself still on grass. The misty elusive pathway still enticed to the left and downhill and after several endeavours I found the rough pathway under my feet and went forward with confidence. If that episode can be laid at the door of the pixies I am grateful to them.

TWO WITCHES OR ONE?

There is an old story about a witch, a very powerful black witch, who lived near the delightful little village of Sourton, which is tucked under the western edge of Dartmoor, between Okehampton and Tavistock. The devil is said to spend many a long hour sitting on the moor above Sourton so that he can umpire the rows which go on between Sourton and Okehampton, with a watchful eye on Tavistock, the enmity between that town and Okehampton being greater still. But to return to the witch, this lady had a husband who became embroiled with the forces of law and order in the late nineteenth century, making an appearance before the magistrates at Okehampton. His wife accompanied him to court and when the man was sentenced, rose in her seat and denounced the magistrates, the clerk and anyone concerned with her husband's troubles. The Chairman should die almost at once, the others at stated intervals. And none should die in his bed. This dire prophecy came to pass. The Chairman died as he was talking to an employee, the others died as the lady appointed, the complainant dying rather horribly as the result of a fire. Even the unfortunate Clerk to the Magistrates who must have played a very minor role in court that day, fell dead from his bicycle as he was riding near Okehampton.

Here is another story, but so similar to the first in fact but so dissimilar in fiction so to speak that one is puzzled to decide if the story is the same story with two different versions.

In 1953 Miss Sylvia Calmady Hamlyn, a lady far more interested in the breeding and welfare of the native Dartmoor pony than in the efficacy or otherwise of spells and spell-weaving, however near neighbours the practitioners of such arts might be, contributed an interesting article to the local newspaper The Western Morning News, as follows:

'It came as something of a shock, after sixty years, to read the brief account given at the Devonshire Association's meeting in Plymouth of the events involving my father's death in

September 1897 ...

'His interests being in London, he only came to Leawood (the family home) for the three summer months, where his stepmother joined us to keep house.

'I was about ten when we first went there and rode my Dartmoor pony a good deal about the district.

'He made me promise never to go on a certain rather poor little farm lying under the Moor ... He told me once that there were bad people called black witches who did harm to their neighbours but that quite harmless old women often got that reputation, and that he and I were going to take soup to one such victim – living in great poverty and isolation, because the villagers refused to allow her to come to the village.

'On September 1st 1897, he rode, as was his custom, to Lifton Court, the other two magistrates being Mr. Kelly of Kelly and a man whose name I forget. The noted black witch had been summoned for the first time by the police for some offence of theft, and the magistrates gave her some fine – my father, I think being in the chair. As they left the courthouse, she stood on the steps and cursed them, giving my father at most three days to live, Mr. Kelly two years and the third man three years.

'Of course Bridestowe village rang that night with the news of the cursing of the magistrates – particularly of "Squire".

'On September 2nd he went out riding about ten thirty a.m. while I was still at lessons. At 12, a frightened tenant came with news of an "accident" to Squire and we waited. At three the Rector came and told us that my father had been found dead, with his horse standing by, at a spot not far from the black witch's holding. He was 44.

'Within two years I was visiting my step-grandmother at Exmouth where she lived, and saw a paralysed, helpless man in a bath chair – Mr. Kelly of Kelly, who shortly died. The third magistrate died within the limit of his curse.

'I did not know the story until, at 21, I returned to Bridestowe ..... when the Rector told me, and added: "I have preached against the power of witchcraft all my time, and after that it was no longer any good." ...'

There we have two stories but so similar that one is possessed with an irritating compulsion to investigate more deeply into both. The first story is of events believed to have taken place in 1896. Were bicycles so common then that the magistrate's clerk would be cycling around Okehampton? Records were being kept in those days and it should be possible to ascertain whether any unfortunate farmer, the complainant against the witch's husband, died about then from burns. Newspapers were already on the scene, and although in intellectual circles witchcraft, unwisely perhaps, had begun to be treated with amused contempt, some notice would have been taken, if not of the witch's curse, of the result of it. But a fair amount of research would have to be done before it could be substantiated that, like that wretched Paul Dupont, the hero of the French primer of my youth, who had not two mothers, but one mother, and needed that obvious fact translated into English, Sourton had not two black witches, but only one.

THE HISTORY OF MISTRESS PAGE OF PLYMOUTH

Having presented the reader with a story of the Kilworthy ghosts in one part of this book it may seem hardly sporting to write an account of what may be nearer the truth about Mistress Page in another. I write, it will be noted, what may be, for I gathered the ghost story of the Kilworthy House from many sources, and I confess that what follows is still hearsay for it is based on a learned treatise by a Doctor Brushfield, written in the nineteenth century. However, this gentleman produces facts and figures to substantiate his claim and the reader, like the writer, is left with a problem. Who are the Kilworthy Ghosts? .. For many a long year we have all accepted the story of the beautiful young woman wedded to the rich old miser, the triumph of love's young dream for a while, then disaster. It is nearly sacrilege and certainly sacrifice to give up these most attractive ghosts. Never has a writer approached iconoclasm with a heavier heart.

That there was a Mistress Page is about all we can rely upon for there seems some little doubt about her maiden name. The touching story of the father sentencing his own child to death is also practically an impossibility for even if she had been the daughter of Judge Glanville, he could not have sentenced her or anyone else for he was not made a Judge of Common Pleas until 1596; he could have attended her trial, however, for he had been in the legal profession all his life.

The ballads and chapbooks of centuries past were the equivalent of our Sunday scandal newspapers, and in an old catalogue issued by a famous antiquarian bookseller, a black letter ballad entitled 'The Lamentation of Mistress Page of Plimouth' was offered for sale. Not only was a ballad made about this unhappy business but a play was believed to have been performed or written by that famous pair, Jonson and Dekker. No copy of it appears to be still in existence but there is evidence that the two borrowed properties and costumes in 1599 for such a play.

The murder for which the four prisoners were executed was committed on February the 11th 1591 at ten o'clock at night, and the executions were ten days later; therefore information contained in a chapbook of that year which is referred to in Dr. Brushfield's essay, is very likely to be correct. In it Mistress Page is accused of trying to poison her husband, and being unsuccessful persuaded one of her servants to murder him. Her lover, George Strangeways, was concerned, as well as another man.

Having decided upon the validity of the murder and the identity of the lady who instigated it, we can look at her background. The 1591 tract states very positively that this Tavistock girl who married the goldsmith, Page, was a Miss Glandfeeld, whose father kept a shop in Tavistock and employed George Strangeways, who seems to have been a great favourite of his master's. There are many old names in Tavistock still, many of them having changed slightly in spelling over the centuries. In one old document Sir Richard Grenville was referred to as "Greenfield" and there has never been any doubt about his identity. There is nothing to marvel at in the alteration of such a name as Glanville.

But whatever the truth of her misadventures may have been, poor Mistress Page died with her co-murderers on the scaffold at Barnstaple. At Barnstaple, because the trial was held there as plague was raging at Exeter where it should have been held, and if murderers were expendable, legal luminaries were not. The three men were buried at Barnstaple but Vlalys Page was taken to Bishop's Tawton and buried there.

THE LADY MARY HOWARD OF FITZFORD

There is evidence that Lady Mary Howard, born Mary Fitz of Fitzford Tavistock, came of intellectual stock for in the early fifteenth century, her grandfather John Fitz, a Governor of Lincoln's Inn was a Member of Parliament for five years and the family continued in importance and prosperity until the ill starred John Fitz was born in the late sixteenth century. There is a story that the young John Fitz's father was a keen astrologer and had consulted the planets as the time for his son's birth grew near. Had the boy's birth been an hour later all would have been well according to the planets, but poor young John was born under an unpropitious star and although his father did all he could no doubt, he died when the boy was only fourteen. Under the appalling laws of that period his wardship was sold to a gentleman, who unusually enough in such circumstances, treated the young boy with great and unwise indulgence. His father had asked his mother to try her best to get the wardship of her son, but she was unsuccessful. He was a good looking lad and probably got much of his own way. Today we should say he had been thoroughly spoilt by the time he attained his majority. Just before he was twenty one he married one of the daughters of William Courtenay and in 1596, when young John Fitz was twenty one, his daughter, Mary, was born.

A few years later, at a large dinner party at Tavistock attended by many neighbours and friends, John Fitz was boasting that he held his lands directly from the Crown and no one else. Nicholas Slanning, a guest at the dinner then remarked that although his family had never bothered to enforce their claim, a small piece of land in the occupation of the Fitz family was Slanning property, but rent had never been demanded for friendship's sake. To the amazement of all present Fitz burst into angry denials, accused Slanning of lying and tried to stab him. Slanning who had a 'great knife' warded off the blow, friends intervened and composed the quarrel and the dinner finished with no more trouble. The party over, Slanning and his servant made for home, the servant leading the horses as his master wished to walk awhile, when they heard a party of horsemen galloping after them. Turning they saw the party was headed by John Fitz. Challenged by Slanning who was astonished at this aggressive encounter, Fitz declared his intention of avenging what he described as an insult put upon him, whereupon all five men fell upon Slanning who fell severely wounded, John Fitz thrusting his sword into the falling man as he collapsed. A servant of Fitz, one Cross or Crosses, has been accused of encouraging his young master in this terrible business, which gives an insight into the weakness of the young man's character. No doubt all the guests were more or less drunk, but as Slanning died, and murder, even in those days, was a serious business, young Fitz had to flee the country. Nicholas Slanning was very popular and was greatly mourned by the Devon countryfolk and Fitz had to remain in France for over six months until the efforts of his mother and his wife gained a pardon for him.

For the next year or so nothing was heard of Fitz except that when King James the First was crowned he was automatically given a knighthood. This probably went to his head for when he returned from the coronation as Sir John he began to behave abominably. First he turned his wife and her small daughter out of doors and both returned to the wife's mother's family where they were kindly received. Then, with a band of rowdy ruffians as companions Fitz and his servants roamed the town of Tavistock, breaking windows and dragging townsmen out of their beds in their drunken brawls. When an officer of the law, presumably a beadle, tried to restrain them, the new knight practically killed the man.

By the time John Fitz was about thirty he was probably a drink sodden nervous wreck, and when he received notice that the children of Nicholas Slanning were claiming compensation for their father's murder it was probably with a coward's trepidation that he set out for London, where the summons was to be heard. Away from his boon companions he began to pay the penalty for his misspent life and as he neared his journey's end he grew more and more troubled. By the time he reached the outskirts of London he was almost a gibbering idiot. Having abandoned his servant he rode until he was exhausted then sought shelter at a small inn. The landlord did not wish to take him in for it was nearly two o'clock in the morning, but the distraught traveller insisted, so the kindly landlord gave up his own room for the visitor. But John Fitz was meeting his reward for all his cruelties. He could not sleep and spent the small hours tossing and turning, crying out that his enemies were pursuing him. Early next morning the landlord who had arranged with friends to cut a field of hay was leaving the house when the noise of a door closing woke John Fitz who by then had fallen into a troubled doze. Leaping out of bed in his night attire he dashed downstairs, brandishing his sword, and killed the unfortunate landlord, under the impression that he was one of the 'enemies' who had come to arrest him. As soon as he realised his mistake and aware of what would happen over a second murder, he turned the sword on himself and wounded himself so severely that he died. Medical attention was obtained for him, but he tore the bandages away, wishing only to end a life which he had himself filled with so much misery.

This tale of horror was the heritage of poor little Mary Fitz. Turned out by her father when she was very small, and but a girl of nine when she became the heiress of a large property, the same accursed law which ruined her father ensured that she was taken away from her mother and her grandmother with whom she had been living, and sent into the care of strangers, for her wardship had been sold by the king to the Earl of Northumberland. The little Lady Mary was twelve years old when she was married to a bridegroom of around thirty, purely as a financial transaction, the little bride continuing to live with her guardian. Sir Alan Percy, the bridegroom, was looking forward to a life of comfort and prosperity on his bride's resources but unfortunately he died only three years after the wedding from a severe chill. This is the first husband the Bad Lady Howard of Tavistock is said to have murdered, but there is no evidence that she was anywhere near him when he died.

Lady Hatton, who had charge of the girl, probably intended her for one of her own young relatives, and many another suitor was pressing for the little widow's hand, and fortune. Lady Hatton was rather unwise to leave the girl behind at her London home when she herself retired to the country for Mary Fitz was then fifteen and, it is said, was very beautiful as well as rich. One evening, in the twilight, Mary escaped from her guardian's house and married the eldest son of Lord D'Arcy. Poor little Mary. Her runaway romance ended in disaster for the young husband lived for only a few months after the marriage. Lady Mary, truly now a widow, and still a ward, was then married at sixteen to Sir Charles Howard, the fourth son of the first Earl of Suffolk. At this marriage complicated settlements were made of the bride's estate which gave her much trouble after the death of this husband, which occurred about ten years after the marriage. By that time Mary had become the mother of two little girls.

At her husband's death it was discovered that her income from her estates was seriously impaired owing to the incumbrances created by her husband on various properties. Long drawn out litigation followed which was settled in Lady Mary's favour in 1628. During this time a military gentleman, Sir Richard Grenville of Kilkhampton in Cornwall and a grandson of the famous Sir Richard Grenville of REVENGE fame, took a great interest in the progress of Lady Mary's financial affairs. When they were brought to a successful conclusion he married her. Mary was by then over thirty but still a great beauty and her estate at Tavistock would be well known to Sir Richard.

Lady Mary was now no inexperienced child. She had had ample evidence of what happens when men marry rich widows, and without discussing the matter with her husband, she created a trust of all her estate, appointing three trustees who – and their successors – should receive all the rents and profits and pay them to her. This arrangement should exist whether she was single or married and it was subject to revocation by a payment by her of twelve pence and due notice.

After the marriage the couple lived at the bride's house, Fitzford, in Tavistock, where their first child, Richard, was born. When however the militarily minded Sir Richard found out about the disposition of his wife's property he was furious. He may have known about the clause providing for the revocation of the arrangement at the lady's will for he tried bullying and ill treating her. He confined her to a small part of her own house. He installed his aunt as housekeeper and refused to allow his wife the management of the household, as Lady Mary complained, the aunt 'ordered and ruled all things.' His foul language and violence towards her increased to such an extent that she was forced to apply to the justices of the peace for protection and when before the bench, he was stupid enough to insult and revile her. The court's protection seemed not to be much use to the complainant for Sir Richard carried on as before, smashing the doors of the house, and threatening her with a drawn sword, ending up by giving her a black eye.

All this was deposed to before the High Court when Lady Mary sued for a divorce. The Court gave Lady Mary her freedom but made her pay for it. Sir Richard was given half her income, which amounted to £350. The divorce was aided by her previous husband's family in the person of the Earl of Suffolk who sent his servant to fetch the lady from her home in Tavistock and bring her to his house in London, where she stayed for some time. This does not look as if Lady Mary murdered her third husband.

Sir Richard Grenville had made a bad enemy in the powerful family of Suffolk. He had unwisely insulted the Earl who pursued him with determination. The Court of the Star Chamber fined Sir Richard £4000 (Insulting the aristocracy came dearer than wife beating) and ordered him to pay a similar sum to the King. Not having £8000 Sir Richard found himself in the Fleet prison. In addition the High Commissioner ordered that he be detained until he should give bond not to offer violence to his wife during separation.

To pile Ossa on Pelion a commission was sent to Fitzford to search the house, as the unfortunate Sir Richard was then being accused of clipping if not actually counterfeiting the king's coinage. Two gentlemen visited the house but ill news travels apace, and there was reason to believe that the servants had been warned. Pincers and files were found, one of which appeared to have been used with yellow metal, and the servants admitted that they had melted silver lace, but nothing substantial enough for evidence for a prosecution was found and the charge was dropped.

Various legal proceedings were taken by which Lady Mary recovered the whole of her estate, which so dispirited Sir Richard that he 'gave himself liberty' and went to Germany to serve in the Swedish Army. He eventually died abroad after many vicissitudes during which he served in Ireland, and on recall, instead of reporting to the King at Oxford, proceeded to London where he asked for and received all his back pay for service in Ireland. He then marched out of London at the head of a Parliamentary force, and deserted to the King, for which he was dubbed 'Skellum Grenville' among other epithets.

Meanwhile Lady Mary had settled herself at Fitzford when she had managed to free it from army occupation. Her son George Howard lived there with her and as the years went by became the comfort of her old age. George Howard married and had a son, but unfortunately he died. In 1671, when Lady Mary Howard was seventy five and expecting her son to survive her and carry on the family name at Fitzford, George Howard also died. The poor woman, worn out with grief at the death of her son, died a month later. Shortly before her death her cousin on her mother's side, a member of the Courtenay family, came from Powderham, the family home to see his dying cousin at Tavistock. He is believed to have exerted considerable influence on the old lady for she left all the estate she had received from her own family to her cousin Courtenay. He was in financial straits for he had nineteen children to support, and it must be remembered that the Courtenay home at Powderham had been Lady Mary's also at a very critical time in her life, when her father had turned her and her mother out of Fitzford. Old age is a time for remembering old kindnesses as well as old griefs, and it must be remembered that although George Howard had been dead for a month when his mother died, the two daughters were still in London. It was the Courtenay cousin who came to her bedside even if his motive in doing so was not entirely pure.

This is the story of Lady Mary Howard of Fitzford, the Bad Lady Howard, who according to the local lore murdered four husbands. It has been taken from a pamphlet written and published by Mrs. G. H. Radford in the nineteenth century. It has copious references to the authorities and sources consulted by the writer, and is certainly more to be relied upon than a work of fiction by Mrs. Bray whose account of the lady of Fitzford, was approved by another nineteenth century writer on the slender grounds that as both lived in Tavistock, even though over two hundred years separated their lives, Mrs. Bray would be a more reliable authority on Lady Mary's history than anyone else. Lady Mary herself has been confused with another Lady Howard who had four husbands and is believed to have murdered at least two of them. She is also believed to have been the child of one of the sisters of John Fitz the elder, and born a Howard. I feel that Mrs. Radford's is the correct history. Lady Howard lived in Tavistock for many years. The details of her life would be well known. Her agent lived at Walreddon and was her trusted friend and confidante all his life. He and his wife knew the lady's affairs as well as the lady herself. Is not the explanation plain jealousy? Lady Mary's wardrobe and cash in hand in the house at the date of her death was valued at £1000. She lived in London for many years, (probably her stay was enforced for she was caught in the early struggles of the Civil War). Her Tavistock neighbours may not have understood her for she was given to study, her books were valued at a fair sum. She was a fine lady and a clever one. She was also a beauty and had succeeded in a man's world. Lady Mary Howard was a natural focus for envious gossip.

BRIDGES (HAUNTED AND FAIRY) AND WELLS (HOLY AND WISHING)

There is a bridge at Tavistock which is the subject of a legend so whimsical that I cannot believe it to be other than a recent fabrication on someone's part. The story goes that the Queen of the Fairies came to the edge of the Tavy and wished to cross. Conveniently ignoring her wings, she took a handful of water and threw it into the air. The drops fell in a glittering cascade, but as they reached the ground the glittering drops turned into pebbles, the pebbles became stones and before the royal fairy lady could say 'Robin Goodfellow' or whatever may be the elfin version of Jack Robinson, there was a substantial stone bridge, over which the Fairy Queen and her train passed to the other side of the Tavy, leaving the bridge where it was, for the use of mortals. Pretty isn't it?

A bridge in Hartland is known as Bow Bridge and is haunted by two ladies dressed in rustling silk garments. No one knows who they were when they were alive and there is not much chance that anyone could recognise them now, for they appear without their heads. There is another bridge in the same area which has a delightful little ghost. It is a small calf which appears there nightly.

Near Stover on the south side of Dartmoor there is a bridge over the river Bovey which is haunted by a strange unidentifiable shape which runs along beside anyone crossing the bridge. The Bovey seems a sadly haunted stream for near the source of the river there is a tiny little bridge which possesses a terrifying atmosphere frightening people into instant flight. On the other side of Dartmoor I was told of a bridge which existed many years ago over a river, perhaps the Meldon, "very high up in the moor" according to my informant, which was beset by a phantom man on horseback. I have not been able to identify this bridge.

An enveloping sensation of human conflict is met by sensitives using a bridge near Gidleigh over the Blackaton Brook, but ordinary folk I have consulted tell me that they feel no effects at all.

Of wells, Fitz's Well, not far from Okehampton Park has a granite cross to identify it. At one time it was believed to have been one of Devon's holy wells of which at the last count there were fourteen. Other authorities hold that it is really a wishing well and has a special influence on wishes made there on Easter Monday, when, years ago, young people made their way to consult it on matrimonial possibilities. There is yet another theory that John Fitz caused the well to be sunk for travellers to use to prevent themselves from being pixy led. Actually the Fitz family owned Okehampton Park in the 16th century and no doubt John Fitz was merely providing a water supply as a good landlord should.

There is, or used to be, for what planning hasn't done these days water boards have, a holy well at Ladwell at Ashburton. The overflow from this well joins the Ashburn river outside the town. This well was known as Our Lady's Well which became corrupted into Ladwell. Then there is Gulwell the water from which was considered to be good for sore eyes. This well was believed to be under the power of Saint Gudula who was the patron saint of the blind. She used to have a cross over her well and fragments of it were to be found until quite recently at a nearby farm.

A very famous healing well at Totnes has, or had, three oblong troughs made of granite, each catching water from a different spout. One trough contained water good for sore eyes, the second, known as the Long Cripple for it is much longer than the other two was used in cases of lameness and also for the bite of the grass snake, which is sometimes known as the Long Cripple. The third was used probably for bathing lepers for the lazar house was close to it, but it is generally known as good for skin diseases in general.

There is a well near Haldon Moor now known as Lidwell, a corruption of Our Lady Well but whatever powers it may have had were extinguished by the behaviour of its infamous custodian whose story is told in the Ghost section.

STRANGE FACTS AND FANCIES

A Story from Dartmoor

There used to be a cross on the road from Plympton to Princetown where Saint Paul used to stand when he preached to the Dartmoor tinners. These gentlemen were a just if tough lot, for it is said that at their stannary courts a tinner who presented adulterated metal for examination, had the sample melted and poured down his throat. Many of the tinners were believed to have been Jews. They found the capital and organised the work, Christian labourers providing the manpower. In return for the concessions King John made the Jews build churches for the workmen.

A la Ronde

There is, or was, a strangely built house near Exmouth, built in a period when people did not build strange looking houses as a habit. It had a thatched roof and its rooms were ranged round an octagonal hall. The doors presented some difficulty so sliding shutters were used instead of the ordinary hinged doors. The mansion was erected at the behest of two maiden laides, the Misses Parminter. Not content with this bit of eccentricity and wishing to benefit females in a similar state to theirs, they went on to design an almshouse and chapel in an adjoining field. This was to be a refuge for four old maids in old age and poverty. Their souls were catered for by the chapel which bore the distich, 'Some Point in View, We all Pursue' – a statement providing a refreshing amount of scope for their old age.

The Misses Parminter must have been ladies of strong convictions. There were some beautiful oaks in the grounds of their conventual benevolent institution, which became known as "Point of View" from the verse over the chapel door. These oaks were never to be cut unless they were needed for making ships to take the Jews in Britain back to Palestine. Now how would the anti-race laws deal with that?

Napoleon's Lock

I do not know if Dunilewy House still stands in Seymour Road in the Mannamead district of Plymouth, but it was in that house in the latter part of the nineteenth century that a door lock needed repair. It was taken off and an inscription found on the back of it which read:

> "This lock was on the chamber door at St. Helena wherein breathed his last he WHO made princes bow and kings to tremble on their thrones – NAPOLEON" ...

The words WHO and NAPOLEON were in German text, a practice in legal documents to emphasise words of special importance. It was discovered that a barrister, who was a frequent traveller abroad, used to live in the house but nothing seems to have been known about his political sympathies.

Future Events and Their Shadows

This story was believed to have been one of the stock jokes of the Reverend Baring Gould. He related that a newly inducted rector of a small parish near Plymouth inspected the register of his new church. Noticing that all the baptismal entries referred to boys he questioned the verger on this parish idiosyncrasy to be told "Dockyard won't take maidens, zur, so waste o' time having 'em christened" ... referring to the necessity for documentary proof of birth required by the Admiralty for employment in the Naval Dockyard at Plymouth.

Seventeenth Century Inflation

Sir William Davenant, the seventeenth century poet laureate, found himself in Plymouth and was horrified at the prices he was forced to pay. He commented "This town is dearer than Jerusalem after a year's siege, and they would make us pay for daylight if they knew how to measure the sun's beams by the yard!"

THE STORY OF TWO RIVERS

Many years ago when even Devon was a very young place indeed, an earth spirit lived in a subterranean country somewhere below what is now the Devon and Cornish border, rather to the north of it. He had a very beautiful daughter called Tamara, but, as beauties often are, a wilful mischievous maiden she was, who delighted in escaping to the upper world whenever she got the chance, despite her anxious father's warning that nothing but evil would come from such daylight trips. He had some justification for this opinion for it was well known that Dartmoor to the south of the maiden's usual playground was peopled with giants. The old spirit gentleman was a true prophet.

One day Tamara was frolicking about in the upper world somewhere between what we call Bude and Bideford, when two hulking young giants caught sight of her from their Dartmoor home and came along to make her acquaintance. They were brothers, massive and masculine and their names were Tavy and Torridge. All three were young and Tamara behaved exactly as all young she things behave. She led her suitors a dance. Over moor and meadow hill and dale, cliff and beach she flitted until the two giants were exhausted. Then she went home. Day after day she carried on in this frivolous manner until either she became careless or the giants craftier for they managed to corner her. She gave in at once and all three sat down to discuss life, upon which subject youth is always so knowledgeable, and such literature as was then available in that early world. Both young giants fell headlong in love with the beautiful Tamara, and at a pause in the earnest discussion they informed her that she would have to choose between them before she went home. At this interesting point in the conversation her father – who had missed his daughter and become very anxious so that he made one of his infrequent visits to the upper world, – came upon the trio. Seeing her seated in earnest conversation with two of the beings he most hated and feared he flew into a rage. Putting an efficient slumber spell on the two young giants he ordered Tamara below. Tamara in all ways a girl of spirit, refused to leave them. Her father snapped the earth spirit equivalent of "We'll see about that", and turned her into a river which should run south, away from the slumbering giants for ever. Weeping bitterly poor Tamara dissolved into a stream which crept away through Devon to the sea.

The Tavy rushing to the Tamar

Not long after Tamara left Tavy awoke. Finding Tamara gone and forgetting his brother, he ran home to his giant father on Dartmoor and poured out the story. The fond father, showing more sense than the earth spirit, comforted his son, but confessed that he could do nothing about Tamara. To console him however he turned him into a river also and sent him running down from Dartmoor to seek Tamara. Tavy, the swift flowing Tavy, caught up Tamara before she reached the coast and together they still flow into the sea.

Poor Torridge was not so lucky. He awoke to find his companions both gone. A wise man who happened to be passing told him what had happened and at his request turned him into a river too so that he could go in search of them. But they had gone for some time and navigation was not one of his best subjects no doubt for he took the wrong turning, and after much meandering and turning and twisting poor Torridge continues to flow east away from his beloved Tamar for ever until he loses himself with the Taw in Bideford Bay.

A SECRET SPELL

There is much in this book about the healing powers of the ash tree and its concern for humanity; here is a glimpse of the other side of the matter. There is no evidence however that the ash tree at Modbury was selected for the piece of malevolence, the subject of this little story, because it was an ash. It happened to be the nearest tree no doubt. It would be interesting to know if the choice was deliberate. What would be more interesting would be to know the story of what happened at the tree, why it happened and who were the actors in the drama which took place so many years before the wheelwright's discovery at Modbury.

This particular ash had been felled and wood from it was being cut for felloes by a young wheelwright. To his great annoyance he found what woodworkers term a 'shake' in what was otherwise an excellent piece of wood for his purpose. Splitting it to find the reason for the flaw he found in the centre an old half ounce phial, firmly held in a cavity of about an inch by three inches. When after much difficulty it was extracted it was found to contain a quantity of black hair, believed to be human, some nail parings, and a little evil smelling fluid. Long years before, some person desiring another's downfall had obtained these odds and ends of body fragments from his enemy, – and one wonders how – put them into this little bottle and thrust it into a cavity made in the young tree. The ash had grown round this bit of macabre mischief and, whether the spell worked or not, kept it safe until the wheelwright brought it to light.

THE STORY OF THE GREY WETHERS

The Grey Wethers are stone circles on Sittaford Tor on Dartmoor. There are many stories about them; some concerned with faithless wives and the punishments awarded them. A prettier story, but one slightly suspect in its perfection, comes from very long ago if we are to believe it.

It seems that long ago a sun worshipper came to live on Dartmoor on Sittaford Tor. The sungod concentrated all his efforts on his lone worshipper on Dartmoor. Miraculously the pasture on the man's holding improved until it equalled the finest fattening pasture in the county. His sheep always dropped twins which thrived equally, each lamb outdoing other men's singles. He grew rich and prosperous until the time came when he began to neglect his service to the sungod who had done so much for him.

The most important festival in the old religion of sun worship took place on Midsummer Day. It was the custom for sun worshippers to sacrifice their finest sheep but as Midsummer Day drew near the Dartmoor worshipper had grown more of a Dartmoor sheep farmer and did not wish to part with any of the fat wethers which were in full fleece and due to be shorn the following week. A neighbour had a few late born lambs and to him went the sunworshipper. Acquiring one of the lambs at a low price he took it home, and on the appropriate day he sacrificed it to the god, thinking that the deity would be none the wiser. But the god had been transferred to Dartmoor as well, it appeared, and had become wise to the ways of Dartmoor shepherds. When his disciple went to look at his sheep that evening congratulating himself upon his strategy, he found them turned into stone. And they are there still. Dartmoor's Grey Wethers.

Prosperity left the sun worshipper. He died and was buried on the top of Cosdon Hill. But every Midsummer Eve his forty grey wethers turn back into sheep and graze until the following morning on the slopes of Sittaford Tor.

There is a kind of postscript to this legend. It is believed that as the sheep were ready for shearing when they were turned into stone, any courageous shepherd could make a lot of money were he brave enough to go to Sittaford Tor, catch one of the stone wethers as it turned into a sheep again and shear it before sunrise on Midsummer Day. This far the task seems child's play. Even a novice could shear a wether if he took all night over it, but the operation included a visit to the top of Kestor for dew with which to sprinkle the fleece which would then turn into gold. Even if this could be done in time, the sting is in-the tail of this undertaking for the shearing must be done with the shears of the dead owner, the sun worshipper, and these were buried with him. Even if the brave fellow got this far he would still have to take the shears to the source of the River Teign and dip them into the water exactly at midnight on Midsummer Eve, before he started operations. All very confusing.

THE STORY OF ORDULPH

They think a great deal of Ordulph and his father Ongar in Tavistock. They are interesting to us as a survival of the old giant stories which seem to be attached to high places, in this instance Dartmoor which rises above Tavistock. The king at the time Ordulph was around seems to have been a crony of the giants, and when his majesty went to Exeter, the giant went with him. This incident is believed to have happened around the year 900 when cities were surrounded by walls with formidable gates in them. Arrived at Exeter the citizens seemed to have taken their time in opening their city gates to the king, so the impatient giant grabbed the gates and tore them apart with his bare hands, putting his foot against the wall and wrenching out the hinges for good measure. To round off the exercise he pushed down a part of the wall. All this frightened the populace out of its wits, and the King was rather upset as well for although he remonstrated, politely we may be sure, with the great bully, in order to comfort the terrified Exonians, privately he swore that the massive hooligan must be in league with the Devil.

Back home in Tavistock Ordulph used to amuse himself by standing with a foot on each side of the Tavy while his huntsman drove the wild animals from Dartmoor towards him. As they reached him he struck off their heads with his knife. A lovable character.

CHALLACOMBE DISCOVERY

A fiery dragon was believed to guard the secrets of a tumulus on this deserted spot but these stories do not seem to have daunted a farm worker who, many years ago, bought a small piece of land near it. The stones in the tumulus attracted his attention and he began taking it to pieces to gain material for building a house. As he dug into the mound he came upon a sort of room in a large oven shape, which present day archeologists readily would have recognised as a kistvaen. It was very strongly and securely constructed but he needed the stone and set to work to demolish it. Breaking into one side he discovered an earthenware pot. Believing he had found buried treasure, he stretched out an eager hand to pick it up. As he did so he heard a sudden loud noise of galloping horses, seeming almost to be on top of him. Startled he drew back and looked around the moor; there was nothing to be seen. The noise had ceased as he rose from his crouching position and, reassured, he knelt once more to his task. Again the noise overwhelmed him and he drew back. Three times this happened. The next time his cupidity overcame his terror, and he reached into the cavity and drew out the pot. All he found in it when he had broken it open, were some bones and a little ash.

From the day of his find, such prosperity as he had slowly and painfully acquired, left him. He lost his sight, then his hearing, and within three months he was dead.

KENWITH CASTLE

Is in North Devon and lies between Bideford and the coast. All around that district the Danes fought when they landed from Wales in the ninth century and fell foul of Alfred's army. Fresh from victories in Wales the Danish raiders confidently expected to be able to beat the Devonians as easily, but at the battles which followed they were slaughtered almost to a man. The Danish leader was a famous warrior named Hubba and he had an equally famous lieutenant known as Bjorn Ironsides. These two fought well but both were killed and Hubba was buried on the shore at Appledore, with a cairn of stones built over him in the northern manner. This was washed away by the sea but the spot was known for years as Hubba's Stone.

Bjorn Ironsides was buried somewhere near a corner of the road just outside Appledore, a spot marked by a commemorative plaque, and known as Bloody Corner. He must have been a formidable character, for there is a story that local inhabitants removed their shoes and crept past the corner in stockinged feet so that Bjorn should not hear them.

A famous trophy which Alfred captured from the Danes was their battle standard known as The Raven. This standard was made in fine needlework by the daughters of Lothbroc and was a magical emblem, for the raven embroidered upon it dropped its wings in a dejected attitude when Danish defeat was imminent and clapped them lustily when the Danes were to be victorious.

THE GUY FAWKES STONE

In mid Devon lies the village of Shebbear, and in Shebbear lies one of the many stones believed to have been dropped by the Devil when he was making a hurried passage by air from one part of Devon to the other. If the church was his target he missed it by a short distance. On the fifth of November when children everywhere are lighting their jealously guarded bonfires and bringing out their fireworks, the grown men of Shebbear gather. First they ring a peal on the church bells, then they go to the stone and with long strong staves, heave it over on to its other side. They then return to the church and ring another peal.

This ceremony, which is believed to ensure good luck for the village is very old and no trace of its origin can be discovered.

FORTUNE TELLING POOL

North Tawton is in a neighbourhood noted for folklore and among its famous places is the soothsaying pool of Bath, the name of the family which provided a famous Justice at the time of Henry the Third. This pool is a large deep depression in the middle of farm land, and it fills with water when it thinks fit without reference to general weather conditions; remaining dry in the wettest weather and brimming when the sunlight pours over the landscape. It is said to be deep enough to cover a horse and rider in the centre. On one occasion the land surrounding the pool was sown to barley and the crop had been cut and stooked ready for carting the following day. Next morning, although the sun still shone and conditions were ideal for the work, that temperamental pool had spread itself far over the field and barley sheaves were floating around on the surface of the water.

The pool is predictable in another sense however. When national disaster looms the Bath pool gives due notice. It filled with water before the death of several kings, including George the Fourth, Edward the Seventh and George the Fifth, and also before the deaths of Queen Charlotte and Queen Victoria, as well as the death of the Duke of Wellington, who was considered important enough for a prophetic overflow.

The (Devil) stone at Shebbear

MR. CHILDE OF PLYMSTOCK

This is one of the famous stories of Devon folklore. I do not like it but I have to include it because there may be those among my readers who would feel cheated if I did not. The lunacy of Mr. Childe annoys me and his gratuitous cruelty annoys me more. I know it is only a story, but think of a man cutting the throat of his horse, and, as some versions of this story relate, a favourite horse at that. There's so much of a horse. It is said that dying of cold is not painful. I would feel much kinder toward his memory if he had written his last message in something other than his horse's blood. Or had lain down to die beside his horse, with no thought for his lands or his miserable soul. And fancy being crazy enough to lose hounds on a place like Dartmoor. Why did he not let his horse take charge. Most horses have a better sense of direction than their riders. But there, had the gentleman shown even a ha'porth of sense there would have been no story of Hunter Childe and the monks of Tavistock.

This man Childe was a landowner on the south side of Dartmoor and presumably a rich man. There was a monastic foundation at Plympton and another at Tavistock, each well versed in the art of adding 'golden numbers to golden numbers' and acres to acres. Mr. Childe goes hunting ... During the day Mr. Childe loses the rest of the field and finds himself alone, cold and lost. He staggers on beside his horse and eventually collapses. Time passes with Mr. Childe and his horse getting weaker and weaker. This is the end, thinks Mr. Childe and before his last gasp, kills his horse (a) to write a message in its blood, (and what was the matter with a drop of his own?) or (b) so that he can disembowel the animal and creep into its visceral cavity for warmth. The message which this dying monster nevertheless possessed sufficient energy to put into dubious rhyme went:

Whoever finds and brings me to my grave,
My lands at Plymstock they shall have.

The scene shifts. A shot of the bursar's room at Plympton. News has come that Mr. Childe, whom no one could discover when alive on the moor has been found dead on the moor. The monks prepare to go after the poor corpse (and the rich lands at Plymstock). Another shot. The bursar's room at Tavistock. A similar company of monks, excited by the news of Mr. Childe's end, (and his sporting bequest) prepares to depart on an errand

Childe's Tomb, Foxtor, Dartmoor *(Western Morning News)*

of belated mercy. (Territorial ambitions as at Plympton). The Tavistock monks get there first and secure Mr. Childe, horse presumably left to rot. The Plympton monks come in a close second. Chagrined they hold conclave. There is a ford down the river. It would be a simple matter to waylay the Tavistock lot there, because they will have to pass over it. They can then acquire Mr. Childe's body. Patiently the holy men from Plympton wait beside the ford. But no funeral procession appears. The crafty churchmen from Tavistock have made a temporary bridge, over the Tavy higher up the river and have conveyed the body of Mr. Childe safely to their own church. The Plymstock land is theirs.

And that, dear readers, is supposed to be the story of Mr. Childe his horse and his lands. Now for the puzzle he left behind. Nearly all the stories of Mr. Childe and his horse and his lands, end with the words.. 'And this bridge is known as Guile Bridge to this day'. Well it isn't.. I for one don't know it. I have tried long and hard to identify this infernal bridge. A bridge close to Tavistock near Parkwood was suggested. Another informant suggested the bridge near the post office, in the centre of the town. I communicated with the powers regulating bridges and roads and maintaining them, and put the question to them. They did not know.

Then there is another question. Many people interested in the story do not know what happened to Mr. Childe's body after the monks got him to Tavistock. A society interested in folklore in Devon has placed a very impressive monument to him up on Dartmoor near Fox Tor, which gives to the casual observer the impression that Mr. Childe's remunerative body is underneath it. This is called Childe's Tomb which strengthens the impression, but hunting in Moore's History of Devonshire I am happy to inform those who may be worried about Mr. Childe's ultimate refuge that according to this authority he was interred in the church at Tavistock.

THE CHAW GULLY RAVEN

A version of the Scottish Highland story of the Water Bull or Water Horse is told of an old mine known as Chaw Gully, near the Princetown Moretonhampstead Road. This is believed to be a very old mine indeed and one containing the very finest tin ore as well as gold. An old raven, alleged to be one of the pair Noah took on board, sits above it, warning would be adventurers not to lower themselves into its depths. Foolhardy miners were said to have done so in the past and when, suspended by a rope, they reached a certain depth, the raven croaked a warning seconds before a stealthy hand protruded from the side of the shaft and cut the rope. Next day the body of the unfortunate miner, minus various bits and pieces, was discovered laid out neatly on the heather. In the Highland story of the Water Horse, the body remains in the depths but the bits and pieces, the lungs and other organs float upon the surface of the loch.

LUSTLEIGH CLEAVE

Lustleigh Cleave is a great place for seeing things and people of the past. A lady riding nearby reported that she had seen a string of richly dressed riders in a gay procession which disappeared at the end of the wood.

A picture of the Dartmoor Perambulation was later shown to her and she declared that the clothes and style of the cavalcade she had seen were exactly the same as those in the picture. It is said that the Perambulation did not pass that way but many people have from time to time seen the same gay procession.

The old lady who some years ago frequently visited the hut circles at the far end of the Cleave saw no gaily caparisoned riders. She had stayed near the circles a little later than usual one evening and it was just after sunset when she prepared to retrace her steps. As she turned homeward a feeling of horror and impending evil swept over her. Her dog gambolling around, stiffened then rushed to her, cowering against her skirts. Looking back she saw small dark shapes creeping out of the ground around the circles. She and her dog bolted for home and never went near the hut circles again.

The story of small statured humans survives all over Britain, generally in high places, oddly enough with stories of giants. It could have its origin in the time of the Saxon and Danish invasions when the small dark native retreated from his richer homesteads to the hills and barren places, creeping out at night to seek food. But it seems hard that the struggle for survival of these poor little wretches should induce feelings of evil and horror, unless one accepts the idea that ghosts are images arrested at times of great stress of persons undergoing such emotions, but surely such an emotion fixing would be felt all the time. We are driven back to the wee dark men creeping in and out of their holes who seem to bring their emotions with them.

SEVEN PREBENDS OF CHULMLEIGH

Chulmleigh is a smallish town in mid Devon with a magnificent church. It has thirty eight little angels decorating the interior of the roof and many many years ago it had seven prebends, which seems a large number. An ancient Devon historian accounts for the excess as follows. A poor labouring man with many children lived in the district. Work was difficult to come by and life was very hard for him and his family. Much as he loved them he decided that the best thing for all concerned would be to go away for some time, so, as the old historian puts it 'He went on his travels'... Alas the poor fellow might just as well have stayed at home if family limitation was his aim for seven years later he returned to the bosom of his family, when his wife was so overjoyed to see him that after a suitable interval she presented him with seven more children at one birth.

The poor fellow was absolutely terrified. Finding a large covered basket he popped the seven newcomers into it and went off riverwards. On the way he met a very inquisitive lady, the lady of the manor. Seven babies even very small ones, make a fair noise, so the lady stopped the man and asked what he had in his basket. Wildly, above the hullabaloo, he swore he had puppies there which he intended to drown. The lady had ideas of her own even if she did happen to be the lady of the manor, and insisted on removing the cover. Indignantly she took the basket from him, rating him soundly for his intended cruelty. To cut an almost impossible story short she found nurses for the babies, educated them as they grew up and turned them into clergymen. Which is how Chulmleigh got.its seven prebends.

A FIELD ACCURSED

Not far from the Cornish border is a piece of land which brings disaster to those working on it.

Many years ago it was a field in good heart growing fine crops of corn. One harvest time the reapers were at work when an altercation broke out among a pair of them. Before he could be prevented one man had hurled a sickle at the other. Sickles were kept razor sharp and the man was killed. The following year corn was again ripe in the field and exactly the same thing happened again; a quarrel, the flash of a sickle, and death. After that, the dismayed owner would have no further cropping in that field. He put it down to forestry and planted young oaks.

The scene shifts to 1963, when the oaks were being cut preparatory to putting the field back into cultivation. No primitive sickle but an efficient circular saw was the instrument of

Chulmleigh and it's Church *(Knight, Barnstaple)*

doom this time. The blade broke into several pieces when the machine was working at full speed and a flying fragment hit a young married man standing beside the machine, and killed him.

LYNTON'S VALLEY OF THE ROCKS

There is a spot in the desolate Valley of the Rocks at Lynton where a detachment of Devon troops came upon a party of Danish invaders, fell upon them and slaughtered them all, giving the little place its name of 'Dane's Glen' but there is a more complicated story of disaster, more or less home grown about this whole devastated region. This story has a slight Teutonic flavour with echoes of Elgar's 'Black Night' but the ending betrays the influence of the English nineteenth century, the virtue triumphant and evil foiled of that period's parables. It is too complete, too morally rounded, but here it is. The reader is judge. Hear then the story of Lynton Castle.

Lynton Castle used to stand four square on this grim northern coast of Devon. It was a busy self contained stronghold as such places were, but travellers came to the gates and were entertained according to their needs and status and one day they were joined by a strapping great monk. He asked for alms but the lady of the castle whose husband was away performing some knightly obligation, was afraid of his gloomy expression and refused him entrance. She seems to have been a shrewd lady for the holy man responded by cursing the place asserting in a startlingly modern political fashion 'All that is thine shall be mine until in the porch of holy church a lady and child shall stand and beckon'. The story gives no account of what happened to justify the monk's curse in the lady's lifetime, but one of her successors an avaricious sort of baron, demolished the early church of St. John and appropriated its treasures. As he sat counting his ill gotten gains the black monk appeared, and incontinently the baron died screaming for help. His servants who flew to his aid, found only his lifeless body.

The baron's son was appalled by all this horror and went off on the crusades which took a long time getting there and back in those days when one was beset with all manner of evil temptations on the road. These last were introduced to the young man by the black monk, who, in the guise of what the nineteenth century would call bear leader to the young fellow accompanied him wherever he went. His mother and sister, strangely enough in those days of tardy communication became aware of the young man's errors in the matters of wine and women, one presumes ill news always has travelled apace, and were so depressed about it all that they simply lay down and died.

Returning to his home at Lynton at last the young man happened to arrive there on a Sunday. The church bells were pealing (someone had no doubt rebuilt the place) and the sound brought back memories of his childhood to the returned prodigal. The black monk, supernaturally informed of his disciple's weakening, appeared at his elbow to whisper of further amorous pursuits which awaited him but lo! in the shadow of the porch stood the shining ghosts of his mother and sister. Shouting of salvation like any transatlantic hot gospeller the repentant crusader dashed toward them, and, seizing their hands, was wafted heavenward. The black monk, thwarted, leaped into a chasm which opened at his feet and the castle crashed to the ground, the great stones from its buildings littering the valley, the valley which is now known to tourists as the Valley of the Rocks.

SIR FRANCIS DRAKE

Born at Crowndale near Tavistock and baptised at the village church at Whitchurch, Sir Francis Drake grew to become among many other things Plymouth's Mayor, Devon's most famous son and Queen Elizabeth the First's 'Beloved Pirate' .. His history is so well known that it seems impossible to learn anything about him that has not been said over and over again. However, when the Tavistock farmer's son became famous he suffered the penalty of fame. Jealousy in the higher echelons of the Queen's court and in Devon society, and just plain idle gossip elsewhere in Devon among people of every degree, soon provided Drake with a reputation earning him a high place in the folklore of the west.

His famous idea of setting hulks on fire and sending them drifting among the Spanish ships to cause terror and confusion was not hailed as brilliant strategy among his countrymen. It was classed as witchcraft for, aided by his own particular demon, he is supposed to have gone to Devil's Point, that promontory on the coast near Plymouth, and cast wooden chips into the sea. The demon obligingly turned them into fireships for his master. It is nice to know that Drake got the official credit for the episode according to the historians. If he had such an assistant Drake worked the poor creature pretty hard, for he is said to have driven from Plymouth to Tavistock on winter nights in a coach drawn by headless horses escorted by outrider imps and a pack of headless hounds, yelling enthusiastically from non existent throats.

Even his efforts to provide Plymouth with water, successful as they were, did not escape comment. Some say he walked, others say he galloped on horseback, but walking or riding, the faithful demon was there also, to draw the water of Drake's Leat after his master.

When Sir Francis acquired Buckland Abbey he got the empire building mania common to successful people in all ages and wanted to build a big barn (the farmer in him coming out, no doubt.) The Devil himself built him one in three nights. Drake's butler was so astonished at the first night's progress that he decided to keep watch the following night so that he could find out how such speedy work was done. Accordingly he betook himself to a large tree near the site and climbing up into its branches being well hidden from below, settled himself to wait. Along came the Devil driving several teams of oxen at once. Now several teams of oxen are a handful for any teamster, even a diabolical one, and these were no exception. Some were sluggish and held back the others, whereupon the Devil got mad, uprooted the butler's tree and leathered the oxen with it. Surprisingly the butler survived the catastrophe but lost his wits as a result and never recovered them.

Many years ago there was a story in Devon that some time after Drake's death, a small room in Buckland Abbey which had been closed for many years, was opened. Inside was a box, sealed and dusty. It looked as if it might contain family papers, so it was decided to send it to the member of the family who had inherited the estate. A carriage was brought round to the door and the box lifted into it. The coachman climbed to the box and prepared to drive off. The carriage refused to budge. The horses strained and the coachman cracked his whip, but all effort was useless. Further horses were brought and put to, then the farm horses, and finally the oxen from the plough but the carriage remained immovable. Suddenly a voice boomed out, apparently from nowhere. The box, it asserted, would never leave the Abbey. Willing hands carried it back into the house and the carriage was driven away, drawn easily by the original pair of horses.

Drake's first marriage, to a girl from Saltash, took place in his youth and is blessedly free from fantastic stories. His young wife died. Years later when Drake was famous he married again, his second wife being a member of a rich and influential family. There is plenty of folklore about these nuptials. Drake, of course, continued to circumnavigate the globe, an occupation which took much longer then than now. On one occasion he was away for so long that his wife felt justified in considering herself a widow and prepared to marry again. There are several versions of what happened then. One story has it that the lady and her husband-to-be were standing at the altar when Drake, who, assisted no doubt as efficiently in foreign seas as in Devon by his devoted demon, became aware of the circumstances. Shooting off a cannonball into the atmosphere it somehow managed to home on the church in Devon where his wife was about to commit bigamy, and, rolling down the aisle, came to rest between the pair effectually putting a stop to the ceremony. Drake arrived by the next tide to consolidate the position.

LUNDY

Lundy is said to have its very own variety of cabbage and there are theories that rabbits came to Devon from there about the twelfth century. Home of smugglers and pirates, due to its useful position halfway between Wales and North Devon, there are many stories about the island but one of the queerest must be that of Miss Fiennes's bird. Celia Fiennes, who was an indefatigable traveller in the seventeenth century, described this creature very vividly. She was in a better position than most people of that time to talk about Lundy Island for it had formerly been in the possession of her grandfather, Lord Saye and Sele. The lady swore that this creature lived partly in and partly out of the water, and in case the reader received an impression of something resembling a half tide rock, she adds that it can be called 'an Amphibious Creature'. Truthfully she admits that she has not seen this thing but that does not prevent her from providing a description of it.

This Amphibious Creature had one foot like a Turkey and one like a Goose – one foot for each habitat, we presume – and it had a unique way of dealing with the troubles of incubation. Its eggs were laid in a place 'where the sun shines' which seems sensible enough, but it set each egg up on the small end and there it remained until 'taken up' by whom or what is not suggested, when, Miss Fiennes asserts 'All the art and skill of persons cannot set it up again so to abide'. A statement I, who have had a fair amount to do with hen eggs in my time, can most readily believe.

Harbouring pirates, smugglers and every description of cut throat it is not surprising that the Devil once thought of domiciling himself in Lundy. He was operating on the North Devon coast when he had this idea so he set about making a causeway from a ridge or rock to the westward of Bucks Mill. This ridge was known as The Gore and the Devil laboured away piling up pebbles and rocks. But the poor fellow never got to Lundy for he broke his shovel after about a quarter of a mile and gave up the attempt.

THE DEVIL'S FOOTPRINTS

This story is referred to generally as The Devil's Visit to the Exe Estuary or similar terms, but all variations agree in one particular, that the devil hoof prints were more like those of a donkey, a donkey with but one hoof, or able to hop along balanced on one hoof, a very small donkey indeed for the prints were between eight and twelve inches apart. This strange creature had moved forward in a straight line, up and down, along and across courts, streets, gardens and fields; over high walls and fences, roofs and haystacks, in country and town, village and hamlet, through gates closed and locked, without displacing anything, over an area of about a hundred miles, extending to both sides of the Exe estuary.

There was a slight fall of snow in the Exe area on the 8th of February in 1855, a Thursday. The mysterious footprints were in evidence on the following morning, indeed there were those, who, when the hubbub began the next day, professed to having been out very late on the Thursday evening and had seen the prints being made by some invisible agency in the snow, in the terrifying manner portrayed a hundred years later in the science fiction film 'The Lost Planet'. The hoof marks were about four inches by two and a quarter in size and observers were struck by the fact that the marks were not equally distributed as would have been the case had an animal of some kind made them. Immediately the conjecturers and those who must have an explanation for anything and everything got busy, – the marks had been made by a bird carrying a donkey's shoe, a badger (although even the most credulous could hardly imagine a badger covering a hundred miles in a night, much less marching up walls and over roofs and haystacks). A vicar suggested an escaped kangaroo, and thoughtful seafaring men resident in the district, remarked on the proximity of the English Channel

Littleham from an old print

and suggested that there were strange things in the sea, which those who went down to it in ships knew very well; some or one of these could have had a run ashore on that snowy February night. Those who examined the prints carefully, noted that there was an imprint in the centre of each, like that which would be made by the frog of a little donkey's foot. More impressionable observers swore that the tip of the print was cloven, no doubt starting the idea that the Devil was at the bottom, or rather the top, of the affair.

A contemporary dignitary referred to the nine days' wonder as 'the superstition of the poor, who thought it was a visit from the Devil' ... but avoided any other explanation. People may have been superstitious but they were not uncourageous. A posse armed with guns and bludgeons set off to track down the strange beast, but after miles of tramping in the cold they gave up the chase. The area affected was bounded roughly by Exmouth, Lympstone and Woodbury on the east and Dawlish Torquay and Totnes on the West and north. At Littleham near Exmouth, the trackmaker seems to have become quite excited about the church. It went all round it and marched up to the door. Although the tracks went straight through some locked gates it seems to have backed away from others and closed doors were ignored. In one instance a ruinous shed was entered by the doorway, the door hanging on its hinges half open, the tracks traversing the building then leaving by a gap in the wall.

The Illustrated London News gave the story great prominence, but the Western Times in its report pointed out that a similar happening took place in the same area five years earlier in 1850. No explanation logical enough to be entertained has been put forward, and we are left with the supposition that the Devil did come to Devon over a century ago.

Inevitably other areas have tried to steal South Devon's thunder, (or its brimstone) and you will be told in the west that the Devil paid a visit to and left his footprints at Hatherleigh before going on to die of the cold at Northlew.

THE STORY OF JACK COO

There is, or was, (in these days of parks and planning one can never rely upon the existence of a building from one day to another) an old farmhouse near the river Dart on the Dart's Moor. Here in those convenient days of yore lived a lad whose job was tending the cattle. In those days young orphans and other children to whom the parish considered it owed a duty, were apprenticed to such masters or mistresses undertaking to keep them and teach them a trade or skill which would maintain them in afterlife. Farmers and their wives were glad to get this sort of assistance and usually treated the young people well, teaching them conscientiously. There is nothing in this story to tell us whether Jack Coo, the lad who is the hero of it, was such an apprentice. Whoever he was, someone or something had need of him it appeared for one evening he ran into the farm kitchen in a great state of perturbation, calling that someone was shouting for him from a distance. Everyone rushed outside to listen. At first nothing was heard but the sound of the river rushing by. Then, far away, above noise of the swift water, came a faint voice crying 'Jack Coo, Jack Coo'.

Here we pause to consider a possible explanation for this story. Has the reader ever listened carefully to the call of a woodpigeon? Would not the sound resemble the name Jack Coo, especially when repeated twice as a woodpigeon repeats the two syllables. Woodpigeons will come where there is food and a tree or two. But we must conclude that all the people in the story were country men and would know the sound a woodpigeon makes. However, the seed of dissension has been sown and we will proceed with Jack's story.

On this first occasion Jack ignored the call beyond a passing interest, but when it was repeated several times in the following days and appeared to be getting nearer each time, the poor lad became quite apprehensive. Attempts were made to answer, but these simply silenced the caller (Which is exactly what would happen if anyone responded to a woodpigeon's cry). But it was not long before the farm people had other ideas. The pixies. These little creatures are reasonably harmless in Devon, but are not to be dealt with frivolously. Time went on until it was early spring. One evening Jack was walking with another man up the river slope in the twilight when from quite close across the river came the well known call "Jack Coo, Jack Coo". The boy turned back and called back in reply. This time the voice answered with "Jack Coo, Jack Coo" (would not a woodpigeon become bolder and more responsive in the mating time?) The boy ran back down the slope, calling back that this time he would find whoever had been calling him for so long. The last his companion saw of him was Jack Coo's small figure in the dusk crossing the stepping stones to the far bank. The voice continued to call for some time then stopped and was heard to call no more.

When Jack Coo did not return a search was made for him but not a trace of the lad or his insistent caller was ever found. There is a well known couplet. "Dart Dart, every year thou gainst a heart" ... This in many versions is believed to have been the cause of Jack's disappearance. I cling to the woodpigeon theory but by proffering the enticement I cannot provide an answer to the question of what happened to the boy's body. He could have fallen in the river but the story suggests that he got to the other side. Surely his companion watched him that far. If the river was in spate he could have been washed away but would have fetched up somewhere. He could have gone running up the far bank and tripped or fallen into a cavity somewhere where his skeleton may yet be found. But I maintain that a woodpigeon started it all.

THE PARSON AND HIS CLERK

The road over the Haldon moor from Exeter to Dawlish was perilous travelling in the days when legends were being created. There are two stories of its dangers in this book. This is the second of two stories.

The fact has to be faced that theory and practice can often be very different and when an ambitious priest travelled over the moor to see his Bishop who was lying dangerously ill at Dawlish in that convenient period known to story tellers as "long ago" – his outward concern was for the unfortunate prelate, but his inward interest concerned his own possible promotion. He had with him his clerk, and the two had travelled the moorland road many times before. The clerk knew the road very well, the priest in clerical fashion not bothering much with path finding when there was someone to do it for him.

Steadily the two jogged on into the night which grew stormy and wet. In the middle of the moor they halted, completely lost, for even the clerk could not decide which way they should take. The cleric grew impatient, then angry as they ranged this way and that. Furiously he raged "I'd rather have the Devil as a guide than you!" The poor clerk was mortified and grew more and more confused as his superior ranted and raved at him, when the situation was saved by a countryman who rode up to them. Learning of their plight he offered his services as a guide and before long they reached the outskirts of Dawlish. As I told you before, it was a stormy night and the courteous guide offered refreshment and an opportunity to dry their clothes at his house nearby before they came into the presence of the sick Bishop. Thankfully the weary pair accepted.

Following their guide into what appeared to be a fairly ruinous old mansion they found an excellent fire blazing on the hearth and supper spread, although a rough crowd of fellow guests gathered round to share it. But the food and drink were good and when the company burst into ribald song the priest and his companion were quite willing to join in. The merriment was at its height when a messenger entered the room. "Hold!" he cried. "There is news. The Bishop is dead". Instantly the two churchmen remembered their errand. "We must begone" cried the priest, who was terrified that some other cleric would be at the Bishop's lodging before him. Dashing from the room they found their horses ready at the door. Their host and his friends crowded round them in farewell as they mounted. But the horses would not move. Whip and spur were useless, nothing would make them move an inch. "The Devil's in the beasts" screamed the angry priest. At that the company around burst into demoniac peals of laughter, screaming and dancing around the frightened pair. A sudden roaring burst into the pandemonium and a torrent of water, rising fast, swirled round the horses' feet. That screaming laughing and roaring was the last sound heard by the parson and his clerk. Next morning the people of Dawlish saw to their astonishment that a strange new formation had appeared in the sandstone of their coast. It was the Parson and his Clerk petrified for ever, and if you do not believe this story, go to Dawlish and the people there will show them to you.

THE CANNIBAL ON THE MOOR

Roborough Down is part of Dartmoor very near to Plymouth and many years ago a ruined old cottage could be seen there, not very far from Maristow Lodge. A rather horrible story used to be told of this cottage which was very badly haunted before it finally fell into a pile of rubble. It was said that back in the eighteenth century when those who had no horse or carriage were compelled to walk, a traveller with two small children was making his way to Plymouth. It was a very snowy day and the children were tired and fretful. Seeing the cottage by the roadside the father asked shelter for the children for a while until he had completed his business at Plymouth, when he promised to return and recompense the old woman for her trouble.

In due course he called for the children but was horrified to discover that she had killed and eaten them. During the ensuing commotion it was established that this miserable old woman had treated many travellers in the same way. The story does not include details of the old cannibal's fate; no doubt she was hanged but she certainly left her ghost behind to haunt the scene of her horrible crimes.

THE BREWING SAINT

St. Dunstan was a very busy saint if we are to believe all that has been said of him over the years. He was an indefatigable brewer and was engaged in this business one day when the Devil happened to pass by. Seeing the saint busy with his mash the Devil retraced his steps and fell into conversation with the saint. Pointing out that by the look of the Devon orchards that year the saint would have little sale for his beer, cider would be so plentiful and cheap that it would be practically given away, he suggested that for the trifling price of the saint's soul he would arrange three good frosts which would put paid to the Devon cider hopes for that year. St. Dunstan seemed interested and stipulated that he should be allowed to name the dates for the frost. He chose the 17th, 18th and 19th of May, the latter being St. Dunstan's own feast day. I could not find out what happened after that but knowing many stories of St. Dunstan and his wiles I feel sure the Devil lost. The Devil seems to take a great interest in fruit for in parts of Devon it is said that blackberries should be gathered by the twentieth of September. The Devil marks them as his own after that date and if gathered by anyone else but his satanic majesty ill befalls the gatherer before the end of that year.

HILLERSDON'S HAWK

A mummified hawk used to be kept at Hillersdon House near Cullompton, and in the fashion of holy relics used to bleed, not at any festival or saint's day, but if war threatened England or any other national emergency occurred. The flow ceased immediately the emergency passed. Unfortunately the hawk had to be placed in store with other belongings of the owner and has not been seen for many years. It was last seen in 1957.

THE GIANTS AND THE GREEKS

We are supposed to owe the account which follows to a Welsh monk, Geoffrey of Monmouth, who, in the twelfth century, was chaplain to William of Normandy. But like the rest of us he had to get his material from somewhere and most scholars agree that his research was done in the pages of the Historia Britonus of Nennius, although he insisted that he obtained most of his information from a book brought to him for translation by Walter Mapes of Oxford, who got it from Brittany. Who are we to argue with a gentleman who became Bishop of St. Asaph? But my money is on Nennius, particularly after reading this story.

Aeneas, that famous hero, influenced by a prophecy of Diana, was moved to send his grandson, Brutus, to seek the island of Albion. He set off, accompanied by Corineus, and eventually landed in England. Actually he found the estuary of the Dart first, and sailed up it to land at Totnes. Here they have a stone known as the Brutus stone which used to mark the place where Brutus was supposed to have stepped ashore. Taking up an appropriate position he is said to have exclaimed "Here I am and here I rest, and the name of this place shall be Totnes' .. After this ceremony the adventurous Trojans split up and set off to spy out the land. In no time at all an army of large and unpleasant giants descended upon them and chased them back to their camp. But the Trojans were stout fellows, and getting over the initial shock, they rallied and marched to meet the giants who were so surprised at this sudden organised resistance that they broke rank and bolted back to Dartmoor.

One of these giants, who in odd fashion became even more famous than Geoffrey who wrote about him, was called Gogmagog. This poor fellow had a wounded leg and managed to get left behind in the rush for the heights. He was taken prisoner and carried back to the camp which by then had shifted to Plymouth. Recovering under the care of his captors who treated their large prisoner very well, Gogmagog was challenged to a wrestling match. Corineus himself issued the challenge and the prize was to be the kingship of Cornwall which in some extraordinary fashion appeared to be in the gift of Gogmagog. The giant was quite willing to try a fall and the two began to wrestle. Back and forth they struggled until poor Gogmagog fell to the ground, exhausted. Corineus pounced on him, hauled him to the edge of the cliff and heaved him over, at a spot known as 'Gogmagog's Leap!'

When the foundations for the Citadel were being excavated near the Hoe centuries later the remains of a gigantic human jawbone and similarly sized teeth were discovered, these naturally were ascribed to Gogmagog. Further support for the story comes from the belief that at one time there was a large picture of the wrestling match carved out in the turf of the Hoe. It seems to have been a no holds barred affair for both figures were depicted brandishing heavy clubs.

Index

Printed and bound by P.D.S. Printers,
Faraday Road, Prince Rock, Plymouth.